*Universities...and
Development Assistance
Abroad*

Universities...and Development Assistance Abroad

Edited by
RICHARD A. HUMPHREY,
Director of Commission on International Education
American Council on Education

Published by
THE AMERICAN COUNCIL ON EDUCATION
WASHINGTON, D.C.

Preface

The past year has disclosed possible new vistas in American public policy for international education. The passage of the International Education Act of 1966 is but one of many evidences at hand. At the same time, attention is beginning to focus upon the twentieth anniversary of the Fulbright and similar scholarly exchange programs, and upon our accumulating experience in providing educational assistance to emerging nations abroad.

Higher education in this country is now in a peculiarly good position to reflect upon the future of international education, in the light of the experience of twenty years of exchange and development assistance overseas. This volume of essays was conceived as a contribution to such reflection, particularly insofar as experience in educational development assistance abroad could contribute to imaginative strengthening of international intellectual communication in future. The Commission on International Education hopes that this volume will serve to focus the attention of colleges and universities on the potentialities as well as the problems of institutional commitment abroad.

The American Council on Education is deeply indebted to Walter H. C. Laves, Lynton K. Caldwell, Alvin Roseman, James A. McCain, Arthur D. Weber, Ralph Smuckler, Edward Weidner, and John Hilliard for committing their reflections to paper, in order that they might be made generally available through this book.

Richard A. Humphrey

December 1966.

Contents

Richard A. Humphrey

The Plane
of Government-Academic
Dialogue: An Introduction

Some fifteen years ago the United States government discovered in the American universities a useful instrument of change in underdeveloped countries. The discovery was institutionalized in the so-called "university contract program" developed by the Agency for International Development and its antecedent agencies. Previously the government had not relied upon American education in quite this way. World War II and its aftermath, it is true, established new levels of government dependence upon academic institutions and their people. Faculty were drawn into the government itself, beginning a major trend toward professionalization and diluting somewhat the image of a "government of clerks." Vast research needs, particularly in the sciences, established a new public dependence upon universities. Intellectual communication with other nations was stimulated by exchanges of senior scholars through the Fulbright and comparable programs. What was novel about the university contract program, however, was the use of *institutions* on a substantial scale in cross-cultural relations.

From its beginning in the early 1950's, the university contract program was in fact developed to work at one of the great political problems of our time—the necessity of "evolutionizing" revolution all around the underdeveloped world. This turned out to be a heady challenge both to government and to its university partners. The collaboration proved to be a difficult exercise in

1

adjustment between public and educational policy; not to say of reconciliation between the ingrained working habits of two established bureaucracies.

A good deal has been written about this joint venture. All manner of surveys of university experience abroad have been reported. Essays, pamphlets, and books have given extended attention to the characteristics of the operation. The uneasy working relationship between government and the universities has been commented upon extensively, most notably perhaps in John Gardner's *AID and the Universities*.[1]

Throughout the literature thus far available, however, runs a preoccupation rather more with the "hows" than with the "whys" of the enterprise. This small volume attempts to notice some of the problems of rationale (or, the "whys"), without neglecting the lessons of operating experience (or, the "hows").

These essays focus, then, on American higher education in overseas development. The "emerging" countries are the setting. A major premise of university programs abroad, and of these papers, is that the development of human resource "capital" is a primary goal of the educational process. For the most part, the authors are American academic men. With their universities, they have been conducting an experiment in transnational intellectual communication, the end-objective of which is induced cross-cultural change.

An equitable evaluation of the university contract program can be made only after close examination of both its public and its educational goals. It has not only undertaken the considerable task of "evolutionizing" revolution. The program has also been called upon to perfect a political-educational relationship.

We do not yet know as much as we need to know about "evolutionizing" revolution. What we have already learned, however, confirms that it is a task of great delicacy, and the investment of resources in it will probably be heavy for a long time to come. Maximum political ferment throughout the underdeveloped world

---

[1] Report from Education and World Affairs in Cooperation with the Agency for International Development (New York: Education and World Affairs, 1964).

not only gave rise to this enterprise but conditions it also at every turn. The setting invites the continuing reflection of both government and its university partners upon the equities as well as the means of induced cross-cultural change.

There is no need to enlarge upon the revolutionary setting. Suffice it to say that it begins and perhaps ends in the disproportion between the affluent and the needy nations. This disproportion is so significant to the fate of mankind that it tends to dwarf other problems that have preoccupied us. The fact that the two-thirds of the world which is predominantly nonwhite finds itself disadvantaged is probably of greater long-range significance than either nuclear potentiality or the East-West confrontation. Indeed, the latter two are inseparable from the former.

The Western World faces a major dilemma in this disproportion. Predominantly white, relatively mature societies, the nations of the "have" complex could elect simply to fend for their status against the newcomers. The alternative is to face the fact of revolution among the "have-nots," to seek to contain it, and to find means for equitably resolving the disproportion itself. The United States has chosen the second alternative, and the university contract program is one of its instruments of containment and rectification. This national policy has given our universities a role on stage squarely in the middle of the principal twentieth century drama.

In taking up this task it became apparent at once that the character of the leadership in the emerging states was to be a prime factor in success or failure. Our ability to deal intelligently with this leadership, and its capacity to lead, were obviously indispensable to the attainment of stable development. It has therefore been of great significance that this emerging leadership, on the whole, is youthful and conceptually immature. Impatience is one of its most distinguishing characteristics, "instant progress" its goal. For the most part, this leadership has been Western trained, and has had ample opportunity to see the disparities between its own peoples and the advanced, industrialized nations. Sophisticated technology and matured industrialization have been hard-won and slowly achieved by the developed states, but the underdeveloped simply do not intend to invest generations in arriving at the same status.

It happens that we share with these nations and their leaders the notion that "education" is their top-priority investment. There are, however, at least shades of difference in our respective goals. The United States tends to gamble that economic and technological progress will increase the chances of orderly political growth, and we not unnaturally envision that growth in the terms of our conceptions of political democracy. There is, however, no necessary ambition among the underdeveloped for our brand of political democracy. They may regard deference to it as the price of economic and technical assistance from the United States, and pay that price. But, it remains to be demonstrated that we can count on the political results we desire *as a consequence of* the educational aid we provide.

It is also important to observe that the educational imperative among the underdeveloped is very close to being an absolute. Many emerging states invest substantially more of their national substance in education than do we in the United States. Furthermore, there are few exceptions to the rule that the key to educational development among the emerging peoples is external assistance. No small importance attaches to the fact, therefore, that such aid is available to the indigenous leadership from a number of sources besides the United States—from former metropolitan powers, other states in Western European and nations in the non-Western bloc. As a consequence, experience has taught the underdeveloped the vulnerability of America to the "cold war gambit." It is hardly surprising that some of these nations have bargained with us stiffly for educational assistance on grounds of the ready availability of alternative sources of support.

This then, crudely oversimplified, is the setting in which the development assistance relationship between our government and our universities has been matured. The backdrop is world political, economic, and social ferment. The aim of the partnership is stabilization. The essays in this volume bear upon both and, as well, upon the nature of the partnership itself.

Perhaps the most significant point to stress about the AID-university collaboration is that it is engaged in highly political business. The emphasis appears necessary since such a political partnership is not inherently congenial to universities. Moreover, the job to be done is further complicated by the nature of the instrumentality for doing it. Education is essentially a long-range, permeative process. In the "university contract program" it is called upon to help solve the short-range, potentially explosive problems of emerging nationhood. The national interest of the United States requires that education succeed. It cannot easily succeed without developing new political as well as educational sophistication. This charge lies equally upon the AID partner.

This small volume illustrates that not a little procedural turbulence has marked this particular government-academic collaboration. The fact that contract negotiations and operations have monopolized much of our attention, however, has obscured far more significant factors making for difficult mutual adjustment. These have to do with the nature or substance of the job of educational assistance rather than the mechanics of doing it. They embrace the respective responsibilities of the two partners. And, they reflect the partners' quite different modes of conceptualizing and decision-making. Future efforts at adjustment should be invested primarily on this plane. There is good reason for believing that new and exploitable opportunity does in fact lie ahead for the collaboration, largely because of past procedural accommodation between the partners.

The new plane for the university-government dialogue stems in part from the following developments. On the whole, our universities have learned to live with the AID "Standard Contract." They might wish it were more flexible, but much less academic energy is now expended adjusting to it than used to be the case. As a result, both the universities and AID can now concern themselves somewhat less with means and mechanics, somewhat more with the substance of the program and the more subtle problems of the university-government relationship. Those long associated with the development of the AID-university cooperation, will not greatly regret the deescalation of the former "logistic" warfare.

Beyond this, our universities are increasingly introspective about their own responsibilities and obligations as educational instrumentalities abroad. They, and the agency, now appear to share a greater sense of long-range commitment than at any time in the program's history, and some optimism about more substantial Congressional support in the future. They look forward to increased financing designed to strengthen our educational resources for continuing development assistance abroad.

Experience has further impressed upon both AID and the institutions the need for greatly expanded research efforts on the conditions of induced cross-cultural change and on the development requirements of specific emerging countries and areas. AID has also evinced an increasing willingness to utilize universities in program planning as well as execution, and it has called upon the counsel of academic country experts more and more in the past few years. These and other advances in the conditions of collaboration now make possible a joint attack upon more significant problems in the relationship.

Ranking high on any list of such problems is the need to appraise prospective educational assistance commitments more effectively in the first instance, in every country or area where an American educational institution is asked to work. Something has already been said about the motivations of the "host countries" in requesting educational help, and about our own purposes in affording it. We have learned some valuable lessons about what must and can be done. But, we have more yet to learn.

For example, we know that the empirical philosophy of the American university, particularly in the sciences and technology, offers something of value to an emerging society. To illustrate, even though much of the leadership of these societies is classically trained, it has come to recognize the pragmatic virtues of a rural development program, the training of engineers or animal husbandmen, the education program in public health, public safety, or public administration. In a decade and a half we have amply demonstrated the value of secondary school teacher training, of research in agricultural science, and of the adequate training of physicians. The list could be lengthened, but it needn't be.

The United States, too, has learned. We have quite well digested the first lesson in the primer—that *indigenous* need should be the determinant of what we do. Advanced principles of crop rotation must be relevant to the host country, for example. They may have been developed in upstate New York, Michigan, or Iowa, but their relevance must be to the Middle East, South Asia, or Latin America. What we know about sound educational administration or simple sanitation may have been derived in practice anywhere in the United States. Our job abroad is to translate it into local experience, not to transplant it. Not a few university contracts have been less successful than they ought to have been because we had to learn by experience to translate technology rather than to attempt to transplant it.

Now, however, AID and the universities confront problems of evaluating country needs on another level of sophistication, one which is politically and educationally hazardous. The second lesson in the primer is that, to be intelligent, initial program judgments of indigenous need must be made by us rather than by our hosts. Even when we can afford it, our interest is not served by acceding to foreign requests for assistance unless we are thoroughly satisfied of their validity. No great imagination is necessary to discern both the professional and political dangers inherent in this requirement. It is not enough, that is, to apply our assistance to indigenous need, difficult as this may be to accomplish. We must now be willing to discriminate between the real and ostensible. We and our "hosts" may differ materially in this assessment, but it is to our interest and theirs to decide primarily on the basis of *our* judgment of their needs rather than theirs.

All experience demonstrates that the educational motivations and objectives of the emerging nations are often remote from reality. On the broadest scale, many developing states are less interested in educational assistance per se than in the political status they believe accompanies it. On the narrower scale, many are compelled more by the symbols of twentieth-century education —national universities, advanced scientific equipment—than by the less glamorous, though indispensable, concomitants of educational development. And, as has been noted, not a few have astutely diagnosed United States vulnerability to the "cold war gambit"—if you don't help us we can turn elsewhere.

It would be a grave mistake for us to be unduly swayed either by the political naïveté of much of the underdeveloped leadership or by resentment of the occasional application of blackmail. Both are entirely understandable. However, our own educational resources are already suffering such heavy overdrafts and the long-range political purposes of our assistance are so paramount, that we can neither afford to share the naïvéte nor accede to the blackmail. Our own best estimates are the only safe criteria for judging the real needs of those we plan to assist. Experience alone perhaps could have taught us this hard lesson, but it should surely have taught us by now.

A second continuing problem in the AID-university relationship is one of sheer communication of the partners with each other. Although on the surface this may appear to be essentially a procedural matter, in actuality it is a good deal more. The fact is that AID and the universities tend to think about international education matters and to organize for action differently. In important respects both their habits of thought and their patterns of decision-making are at odds.

As most government agencies charged with international responsibility, the Agency for International Development plans and manages primarily in geographical terms. The key conceptual framework is the "country plan," developed within the overseas mission setting. The effective foci of decision-making are: in the field the ambassador, and in AID/Washington the regional bureaus, in the hands of "country desk" officers. By contrast, the academic community tends to think and act within the framework of "disciplines." Its research, teaching, and patterns of action are bounded by the substance of learning and it identifies its practitioners within these boundaries. Anyone can at once name exceptions to these generalizations, but on balance the exceptions appear to prove the rule.

From the initial discussions of a university contract on through to the evaluation of the results, these difference in outlook and habit make for a difficult collaborative "fit." The academician visualizes foreign assistance needs, for example, as an animal husbandman, an engineer, or as a professor of education. The American ambassador or the AID officer conceives of educational assistance as only one segment of a broad United States support pattern. That pattern is itself conditioned, in turn, by political considerations within a particular foreign country or region, and it is evolved with the national interest both of the United States and the "host" country in view. At best, the government man thinks of academic disciplines in a secondary sense. His university colleague, on the other hand, is normally aware of total country needs only in a secondary sense. This difference in orientation creates a basic difficulty in plugging the university into the government decision-making grid, and vice versa.

Since the whole program operates within a highly "politicized" setting, the search for mutual accommodation in this particular takes on a great deal of importance. To be effective abroad, the university contract man must learn to add to his competence a broader language of thought and action, the political. It is, in truth, a "second" language, for his success obviously depends also upon his substantive expertise. To be effective with universities, on the other hand, AID must strive to look beyond the academic expert to his expertise, and to plan and act in the light of learning's relevance to politics. Gardner had this in mind, it seems evident, when he stressed the need for AID to attract "able professionals" and to create "an environment in which they can function effectively." [2]

A third residual problem in the relationship similarly has to do with divergent habits of thought, as well as with substantial differences in the pressures which motivate the two partners. The pressures on government have much to do with setting its patterns of thought and action. Two very different pressures bear particularly on AID: (1) the revolutionary backdrop against which the whole AID role is played out, and (2) domestic reactions to its programs, which require the practicing bureaucrat at all times to be ready with "evidences of effectiveness" for a suspicious

[2] Gardner, *AID and the Universities*, p. 31.

Congress and general public. The effect of these pressures upon the AID-sponsored university programs abroad surfaces as a government demand for visible, readily measurable, essentially *short-term* results.

Such a demand is not only uncongenial to academicians, it will not equate with the nature of education itself. Education is a process rather than a product, its achievement is permeative and *long-range* in character, and it cannot easily be "measured" in terms satisfactory to a member of Congress, an AID executive officer or an accountant. Quite aside from this, the setting within which universities labor abroad and the purposes for which AID depends upon them, militate against visible, readily measurable, essentially short-term results. Nevertheless, AID's clients (the emerging countries assisted) and its backers (the Congress) continue to press for the "product" which it is exceedingly difficult for education to produce.

There is no facile answer for assuring greater accommodation between such opposing instincts. One course, obviously, is for the academic community more effectively to persuade its sponsors of what education can be expected to accomplish in an alien setting. In so striving, education has new public acceptance on its side and can base its missionary efforts for better understanding on this fact. It will also be necessary, however, for universities consciously to seek accommodations in the educational process itself, and strive for adaptations to the new cross-cultural challenge. Although basically conservative, education has met such challenges before under pressure of public necessity—as in the perfection of new language training techniques. In any event, the issue of short-range versus long-range motivation must be composed if we are to be serious about the university contract program as a continuing commitment.

A fourth residual issue, startling at first glance, has existed since the beginning of the program. There are at present virtually no mutually agreed criteria by reference to which AID can choose competent institutional collaborators. The selection of university contractors has tended, rather, to run heavily to those in whom the agency has had confidence by virtue of their previous experience in the program. The university resource-base is, accordingly, relatively restricted; AID is vulnerable to charges of favoring a few among many; advantage is insufficiently taken of the interests and competences of other institutions; and the universities themselves lack a frame of reference which would facilitate their own judgments of capability.

The need for excellence in university performance overseas is not an issue between AID and the academic community. Experience has amply confirmed in this matter what principle dictates, and perception of what constitutes excellence has steadily broadened since the beginning of the program.

We know a good deal, for example, about the resources an institution must be prepared to deploy abroad if it is to be successful in the public service. And, we know that our calculations must take as sharp account of quality as of quantity. Theoretically, an open faucet of government support to universities would, in time, solve the problem of quantity. It would not, however, guarantee faculty of first quality for the sensitive overseas task. At whatever level of professional attainment a university utilizes faculty on its AID contracts, they must be the most able it can offer.

Yet, from a university's point of view, a commitment to utilize only its best men abroad cannot always be matched by ability to release them from the home campus. Elusive factors enter the equation, not easily measured much less codified in criteria. The "seriousness" of an institution's commitment, for example, may be essential to an appraisal of its capacity, yet nearly impossible for AID or even the university itself to judge. Institutional "interest" is obviously indispensable to a first-class performance in an arduous alien setting, but it may be no gauge at all either of its corporate capacity or even of its judgment in offering its service to AID.

From the agency's vantage point, on the other hand, it is a safe rule of bureaucratic life that qualitative judgments of potential academic contractors are extraordinarily risky; to be avoided rather than courted by the government officer. Whenever a selection assessment can be quantified, or founded upon proven experience, the risk of later pressures against the selection decision is obviously reduced.

Risks for the agency are also compounded by the folkways of Congress. When AID annually enters the pit of authorization and appropriation on the Hill, scarifying questions are asked about its very existence. At the same time, no one would expect members to be disinterested in their constituencies when, after the din has subsided and appropriations are available, university contractors are selected. It is scarcely surprising that the agency has not rushed into a structured plan for passing qualitative judgments on potential university partners.

Still, the nettle is now being grasped. AID has mounted under contract a special study of the problem, and requested its advisory committee of university presidents to give it priority attention as well. The study and the recommendations of the advisory committee will, hopefully, provide the agency with a firmer and more defensible basis for selection of its university partners.

As is amply shown in one of the following essays, sound evaluation of the results of a university program abroad has been a matter of major concern to both parties from the start. One aspect of this matter which is too seldom discussed is perhaps worth preliminary comment.

That AID is heavily conditioned by its domestic controversiality is obvious to all. Among others, this fact has contributed to the "purchase" psychology which has characterized the agency's approach to universities as well as to other contractors.

By its own lights, AID is on firmest ground when it can contract for tangible "things" or for measurable services. Congress and the general public can recognize a dam when they see one, for example, and a shipment of wheat is quantifiable. The results of the educational process, however, are not easily subject to precise measurement at home much less abroad. As a consequence, AID is frequently at loss to justify what it has "purchased" in a university contract. The dilemma is not relieved by the fact that the special circumstances of overseas development assistance impose their own intangibles for any evaluator of university performance.

How, in fact, can AID discharge its fiscal responsibility in the eyes of a brooding General Accounting Office and a wary Congress if the university "product" cannot be quantified or measured in terms congenial to the standard audit psychology? Even though the tax dollars it invests in universities account for a relatively insignificant portion of its appropriation, how does the agency defend today an investment in university achievement if that achievement can only be adequately judged by the next generation? Indeed, how does either partner cope with the ever-present auditor if unforeseen but controlling circumstances in the host country can completely alter in mid-flight the agreed benchmarks for a university assistance program?

Answers to such questions are unlikely to be found through attempts to quantify the educational process. Clarification of that process, instead, should be the aim of educators. That education is an instrumentality of unique characteristics and values may be generally agreed. Its uniqueness is not on that account, however, self-evident. Illumination of whatever claims to uniqueness education may possess will alone promise modification of the AID "purchase" psychology. Educators should face this task. For its part, government must rest easier in the future than in the past with nonquantifiable judgments of university contract performance. The Congress, for example, is steadily enlarging its support, and understanding, of education. As a result, the agency's opportunities to broaden Congress' comprehension of overseas educational assistance, and the role of universities in providing it, have increased. AID need not be reluctant purposively to encourage communication between the Congress and its university contractors. The agency's advisory committee, for example, is largely made up of university executives of wide experience in the foreign setting. These men and others like them are in an extraordinarily good position to provide the Congress with new insights into the nature of the educational process, and the intricacies of translating it into transnational situations.

Probably no issue more profoundly affects the AID-university collaboration than that posed by the juxtaposition of political sponsorship, on the one hand, and the tradition of academic-institutional independence, on the other. American universities have historically resisted domination by the publics they serve. The marked increase in the interdependence between government and the universities during the last decade in particular has not deadened the sensitivity of the academic community to the problem of "political control." Much of the opposition to the now massive proportions of federal support to higher education has been based upon the fear of political impingement upon academic freedom and institutional autonomy.

The AID-university relationship, however, invites a fresh look at the issue—alike by government and the universities, but especially by the latter. The support, and practice, of educational "overseasmanship" invests the issue with new overtones which should be squarely confronted by all concerned.

A starting point for reevaluation is an inquiry into whether the public purpose which underlies AID support itself compromises the freedom of the university partner.

We need not labor over *whether* public purpose underlies AID overseas programs. It does, or the programs would not exist. In this sense, an instructive definition of "political" would equate it with "national interest" and, indeed, this is the broad conception within which universities should consistently view their overseas missions. In this sense, everything a university or a scholar does abroad under government subvention is "political" in import. Indeed, such are the public stature of both academics and their institutions in our time, that the same might be said whether or not official sponsorship accounts for their presence in other countries.

The real problem, of course, lies in the definition of public purpose or national interest, in the fact that the burden of defining either lies inescapably with government, and in the ultimate responsibility of government for policing its own definitions. Here lies the fertile field for controversy with the university partner, when the latter either (a) disagrees with government's definition or (b) believes that it contravenes academic freedoms or autonomy.

Resolution of these differences cannot easily be achieved

through compromises which cannot be made. For example, institutions would do better to stay clear of overseas AID operations if they cannot, in conscience, accept government's definitions of purpose or its final responsibility for the state of our relations with the countries within which they may work. These are not really negotiable matters, or elements in the relationship. In the end, it is a "ground rule" that Washington, or the American ambassador in the field, will determine on both points, and there is no real intellectual or practical appeal.

Universities cannot, then, argue for unlimited freedom of action or autonomy in government-sponsored programs abroad. This is a stark fact which presumably persuaded John Gardner to speak of "reasonable autonomy" for institutions, in his *AID and the Universities*. The rule of reason says that universities contracting with AID must expect to yield portions of their cherished independence of action—because they labor in a political situation. If this concession is unacceptable to any institution, the alternative is clear—to avoid the political, or national-interest, assignment in the foreign relations field. It is profitless to argue that it is not, or should not be, a political assignment.

Difficult as this may be, however, this adjustment may be more easily made on the institutional, than on the individual scholarly, level. Of the many illustrations which might be cited of potential confrontation between public policy and academic independence, one of the best lies in the area of scholarly publication, such as may result from participation in a government-supported overseas program. In AID's case, the agency specifically reserves some rights of control over such publication. This control obviously touches both institutions and their faculty at an extremely sensitive point. AID is fully aware of the sensitivity on the academic side, but consciously runs the risk because of its own political responsibilities.

Scholars are attracted to AID-university operations overseas in part because of research opportunity. Freedom of the individual scholar to publish the fruits of his research is, of course, a cardinal rubric of scholarship, a rubric no university can itself abridge with impunity.

The milieu within which the scholar works when associated with an AID-sponsored contract, however, is one of great political sensitivity. Because it is, the agency has responsibilities in two directions the discharge of which invites limitations on a scholar's right to publication: (1) the area of national security, and (2) the area of international comity. AID, therefore seeks to prohibit publication which would violate the former, while controlling publication which would disturb the latter.

The fact is, of course, that scholarly publication *can* violate the national security and/or seriously disrupt our relations with other nations even though national security is not specifically involved. In the end, neither the university nor the scholar is accountable. The agency is. In the end, also, the agency must make the judgments. From its point of view, AID cannot "negotiate" with universities or their men either its responsibility or its judgment in the area of scholarly publishing under its contracts.

The research-minded scholar, however, is loathe to repose in AID ultimate decision on what he shall or shall not put in print. The scholar has professional integrities to uphold. Furthermore, he has no assurance that a "national security" ruling by the agency, or an official admonition that what he proposes to publish may seriously damage our international posture, may not in fact merely cloak official error or cover official embarrassment.

Even superficial examination suggests that these differences of view will be difficult to resolve. If resolution is impossible, or nearly so, at least greater accommodation must be sought.

All agencies of government are morally and legally charged with promoting the national interest and protecting the national security. Any agency of government would be culpable were it to fail to exert all reasonable efforts to carry out this mandate. Few federal functions are more complex or genuinely sensitive than foreign relations. Scholars are not immune to error or even irresponsibility, certainly not in putting into print what they judge to be the truth. In the field over which AID presides the potentialities for compromising the national interest by scholarly error or irresponsibility in print are genuinely awesome.

On the other hand, no government official, agency, or policy should be immune to criticism in a practicing democracy. Conscientious scholars should possess at least as much right to criticize as anyone else, and competent researchers in their areas of special expertise should be zealous to exercise this right. The fact that contract-related research is supported by AID funds should not, per se, temper scholars' search for truth nor their right to speak it when they see it. Even in the field of foreign relations, it is arguable that federal censorship to prevent, for example, offense to corrupt or incompetent foreign governments, can actually defeat the larger national interest. In any event, governmental tampering with any genuine aspect of academic freedom can open up a Pandora's Box of woes potentially disastrous to democratic values as we have come to understand them.

The fact that these two positions appear so nearly irreconcilable perhaps illustrates a truth vital to both parties. It is that the program can founder upon the perfectly defensible but dichotomous positions of either partner, and that where their respective interests conflict new and imaginative accommodations must be sought.

AID should pay any administrative or political price to assure that its rulings on scholarly publication are in fact genuinely national interest or security rulings; and should disclose to its academic colleagues wherever possible the reasons for its decisions. For their part, scholars should reexamine the integrities at stake in publishing in the international arena; comprehending that truth is not necessarily denied for lack of public disclosure and that the public interest may in fact be critically compromised unless the option of sound discretion remains open.

These, then, are some present issues which will be amplified in the papers which follow. The success or failure of United States foreign policy, not simply of our universities abroad, will greatly depend upon their resolution.

Walter H. C. Laves

University Leadership in Transnational Educational Relationships

This volume is concerned with a variety of problems that have developed in the relations of American universities and the federal government in the area of transnational educational affairs. Many of these problems have arisen in connection with administration of university contracts to provide technical assistance. The more fundamental questions, however, concern the future respective roles of government and higher education in achieving a deeper American involvement in the worldwide development of educational, scientific, technological, and broadly cultural resources.

During the past three decades the cooperation between the so-called "private sector" of higher education and various agencies of the federal government has rapidly increased in the international area. It is likely to increase even more rapidly in the future, provided international tensions and crises are kept within limits short of nuclear conflict. Indeed, this kind of private-governmental cooperation is part of a growing new dimension in the conduct of American foreign relations which includes activities in education, information, science, culture, and many kinds of technical assistance.[1]

[1] American Assembly, *Cultural Affairs and Foreign Relations,* edited by Robert Blum (Englewood Cliffs, N.J.: Prentice-Hall, Inc., 1963). Charles A. Thomson and Walter H. C. Laves, *Cultural Relations and U.S. Foreign Policy* (Bloomington: Indiana University Press, 1963). Philip H. Coombs, *The Fourth Dimension of*

As one looks back over these comparatively recent developments in relationships between government and higher education, it is clear that they have resulted primarily from governmental initiatives. But in the light of past experience and considering the nature of world needs, it also seems clear that a much greater initiative by the private sector (in development of transnational educational activities) is both desirable and probable in the future. The private-governmental cooperation in such matters should become increasingly a partnership which permits easy accommodation of both private and government interests. There are signs of progress in this direction.

The governmental initiative that has resulted in growing university involvement has been motivated very largely by considerations of foreign policy rather than by any desire to promote scholarship in the United States or to strengthen the world community of education and scholarship as such. Yet, these demands of government upon the academic community have brought about a more universal orientation of American universities and have laid the foundations for stronger educational institutions abroad with which American institutions can collaborate in a world community of education, science, and culture.

It is worth recalling that some of the more important governmental initiatives were related to the conduct of the second world war, such as the development of greater competence in language and "area" knowledge and the attempt to replace German cultural, economic, and political influence in Latin America. Some related to completing the war effort, as in the educational aspects of the postwar occupation of Germany and Japan. Closely related in time was assistance under the Marshall Plan for the scientific, technological, and managerial rehabilitation of Western Europe. The "Point 4" program extending development assistance to underdeveloped regions outside Western Europe was undoubtedly the governmental initiative with the most far-reaching implica-

---

Foreign Policy: Educational and Cultural Affairs (New York: Council on Foreign Relations and Harper and Row, 1964). Charles Frankel, *The Neglected Aspect of Foreign Affairs: American Educational and Cultural Policy Abroad* (Washington: Brookings Institution, 1966).

tions for the world's educational community; it has brought promise of the longest term involvement of American educational institutions. It has provided the greatest opportunities for large-scale institutional cooperation between the federal government and universities and, necessarily, it has contributed to the principal problems discussed in this volume.

In different degrees and in many different ways, all of these governmentally initiated programs called for contributions from the educational community of the United States in the form of personnel, research, new teaching responsibilities, and public service. Whatever contributions the educational community has made to the furtherance of governmental objectives, the major consequence for higher education was that large numbers of university personnel were encouraged to broaden their intellectual horizons and to become more deeply involved in transnational educational relationships. By the middle 1960's, not only individual but also institutional horizons of the academic community had been significantly widened. There have developed substantial numbers of transnational institutional as well as personal relationships that are likely to endure and that already constitute an important element in the world community of education and scholarship.

To the postwar influence of governmental programs that were motivated primarily by political objectives, one must add the impact on higher education of certain other governmental activities which included from the start more direct interest in promoting ideas and values of the academic community. These included the Fulbright program, certain of the United States information activities, the United States-Soviet cultural agreement, the NDEA Title VI program for strengthening foreign language training, and various other efforts toward strengthening the educational and cultural dimension in the conduct of American foreign relations. Unlike the governmental initiatives mentioned earlier, these more directly and more deliberately concerned the longer range development of the worldwide educational community as well as the promotion of international understanding. They often tended to focus upon providing opportunities for individuals as scholars, students, teachers, or specialists to broaden their competence and vision. But, they contributed as well to the broadening of intellectual horizons and the strengthening of academic resources in the institutions from which scholars and other specialists were chosen. Now, there is the new International Education Act and the development of a Center for Educational Cooperation, both the legislation and the center to be concerned with broadening the horizons of United States higher education and promoting a world community of education and scholarship.

Finally, one should note the governmental initiative in the establishment of a variety of international agencies, including UNESCO and other specialized agencies, and regional enterprises such as the Alliance for Progress, all of which to some degree have led to involvement of the American academic community.

Other papers in this volume discuss in greater detail the impact that various governmental initiatives, especially those involving technical assistance, have had upon higher education in the United States; there is, therefore, no need to attempt an evaluation here. It should be emphasized, however, that other factors, notably the programs of certain foundations, have also influenced the direction of institutional and personal professional development during these years and the strengthening of the world community of higher education. These and the governmental efforts have complemented each other in many ways. Their relative importance is not germane to this particular discussion.

Whatever the specific impact of the governmental initiatives and whatever the relative importance of governmental and foundation assistance, it is exciting to observe how large segments of higher education are taking advantage of the new opportunities which the events of the last thirty years have made possible. Increasing opportunities for students to learn about the larger world through comparative, area, international, and foreign language studies, often with related chances to study abroad; increasing numbers and proportions of faculty with foreign and international experience and associations; increasing direct exchange arrangements with specific universities abroad; and increasing enrollment of students from abroad—all of these are becoming common characteristics of more and more American universities and colleges. They have become criteria for judging the dynamism within individual educational institutions and their promise for future growth. The rate of such institutional adjustments is, of course, still uneven and often slow and discouraging; and there continue to be quiet backwaters that have remained relatively unaffected by these mainstream developments of the last two or three decades.

The important thing is that so many institutions, their administrators, and faculties are increasingly taking initiatives, often in cooperation with other American academic institutions and foundations, to extend their world relationships and to reorient and strengthen their own campus resources. This continually growing initiative within the community of higher education itself is already affecting the relative influence of government and the private sector in the development of transnational educational relationships. Though the need for federal financial support continues and even increases, the time is at hand when one may expect much more leadership and direction from the private sector in its continuing cooperation with governmental efforts.

The fact that at the same time educational resources in other nations, both developed and newly developing, have been growing significantly in strength and in their international orientation increases the chances for cooperative endeavors by American higher education with institutions in other nations toward strengthening the world community of higher education.

The growing opportunities and prospects for leadership by American higher education in relation to the combined interests of the governmental and private sectors, when viewed in the context of growing transnational and educational relationships, suggest that a kind of pivotal role may be emerging for American higher education. It is a role which on the one hand involves a partnership with the federal government in the national interest, and on the other hand involves a relationship with the world's educational community in the interest of universal educational, scientific, and cultural values. This is not an easy role to play, because absolute mutual confidence is basic in each relationship. The integrity of each relationship must be maintained with care lest one unnecessarily or unwittingly prejudice the other.

Are there any guidelines which might serve the private sector as it further seeks to adjust responsibly and constructively to this emerging dual role in the world community of higher education? The suggestions which follow are not intended to be in any order of importance, and they are not presented as a blueprint. They perhaps represent points of view from which it seems desirable that American higher education should see its transnational involvements and on the basis of which its policies should be developed.

1. It is basic that American institutions of higher education see themselves as integral parts of the world's educational and scholarly resources. The efforts we make to strengthen these resources and to interrelate them need to be viewed as part of a worldwide effort undertaken not unilaterally, but rather in association with other nations and their educational institutions.

2. It is important that all parts of the American educational community become engaged in the worldwide enterprise. All our institutions should be keenly aware of the influence which events during the last two or three decades have had upon so many, but by no means all, educational institutions in the United States. The hope for such a greater involvement of the entire American community of higher education was reflected in the Morrill, Nason, and Gardner reports [2] which sought to extend the international reach of colleges and universities. It has been the objective of much of the effort of the American

---

[2] *The University and World Affairs,* A Report by the Committee on the University and World Affairs, J. L. Morrill, chairman (New York: The Ford Foundation, 1960). *The College and World Affairs,* A Report by the Committee on the College and World Affairs, John W. Nason, chairman (New York: The Hazen Foundation, 1964). John W. Gardner, *AID and the Universities,* Report from Education and World Affairs in Cooperation with the Agency for International Development (New York: Education and World Affairs, 1964).

Council on Education and the National Association of State Universities and Land-Grant Colleges. This is the primary mission of Education and World Affairs. The involvement resulting from such impacts should be as broad as is possible and should affect curricula, faculty, students, and administration.

3. American higher education should press the government to achieve coherence in its several kinds of support for transnational educational relations—notably, the programs of the Department of State, the Agency for International Development, and the proposed new program in the Department of Health, Education, and Welfare. The universities cannot otherwise effectively relate themselves to the governmental initiatives nor provide effective leadership themselves.

4. A major objective of the private sector should be the strengthening of resources in American educational institutions for teaching about the nature of the world community and the responsibilities of the United States in it. This is of importance not only for educating students who wish to go into international activities, but also for the mass of students needing better preparation to perform responsibly as citizens in a world community. Several federal programs, especially the International Education Act, provide means to assist institutions of higher education in this respect. At the graduate level universities should increasingly provide opportunities for specialized training and research that will assure a growing supply of teachers, prospective public officials, and informed citizens capable of working effectively in transnational and international enterprises.

5. Of continuing concern to American higher education is strengthening educational institutions and research facilities in other countries. American institutions must increase their capabilities for giving continuing assistance to developing nations by lending faculty for overseas assignments and by providing specialized training in this country to help develop faculties and other personnel of foreign institutions.

6. Since the development of educational resources in under-developed countries is a matter of worldwide concern, American higher education needs increasingly to associate itself directly with institutions in other developed countries to provide this kind of assistance. It should encourage the federal government to facilitate these relationships.

7. American higher education should continue to work for increased opportunities for exchanges of scholars and students in order to knit more closely the community of scholarship among nations.

8. There is need for more centers in the United States and throughout the world, in which genuinely collaborative multi-national groups can engage in research. There is particular need for multinational research on problems of common concern: for example, urbanism, human resource development, community development, nutrition, population pressures, immigration, housing, food, and water resources are all problems of multinational concern to which the best of the world's intellectual resources need to be applied in common efforts. American universities ought to provide continuing leadership in this respect.

Developing closer relationships between such multinational research enterprises and the central policy organs of the United Nations and its specialized agencies would help to bring the world's restored resources into the service of the world community and might incidentally reduce somewhat the burdens upon the international secretariat.

9. A major continuing objective of American universities should be the increase of intellectual contacts with politically isolated nations such as the U.S.S.R. and continental China, so that their educational institutions may ultimately become effective participants in the world community of higher education. One factor in developing this kind of communication is increasing teaching and research concerning politically isolated nations and their cultures.

10. The higher education community in the United States

should be especially concerned about strengthening the non-governmental international professional organizations such as the International Council of Scientific Unions, the International Political Science Association, the International Council for Philosophy and Humanistic Studies, and the Eastern Regional Organization for Public Administration. Through the publications and meetings of these organizations professional communication is stimulated and the community of worldwide scholarship strengthened. In addition, a kind of worldwide leverage is provided for scholars and universities, especially in underdeveloped regions, but also in those countries which restrict freedom of inquiry toward achieving higher standards of scholarship at home. Nongovernmental organizations of this kind are as essential in the development of the international community of higher education as they have been in professional development within nations. They can provide important support within nations for such values as freedom of inquiry, freedom of speech, and equality of educational opportunity.

The dual role that has been described as emerging for American higher education with its national and transnational responsibilities poses problems for its partnership with the federal government. There is no getting away from the fact that the federal government must be continually concerned with the foreign policy implications of programs it supports. These may be broadly international, regional, or very much focused upon relations with individual nations. The promotion of the multifaceted national interest within the world community of nations must be its dominant concern. In equally general terms the universities are committed to the values inherent in teaching and research. These are essentially timeless in nature and are the unifying concern of scholars and teachers, not only within the United States, but in the world community.

The success of the partnership hinges first of all upon the capabilities and mutual confidence of persons who are involved in maintaining the relationships between government and the private sector. Secondly, it depends upon clear recognition by both sectors of their respective appropriate functions and of their respective competencies. Thirdly, it depends upon a clear recognition of the values, both common and differing, that must guide the government and the universities, respectively. Neither can be permitted to corrode the credibility of the other. Finally, it continues to depend upon the suitability of patterns of organization within both sectors for carrying on effective collaboration.

There are many indications that the partner relationship between the federal government and the universities in transnational educational programs, for which new foundations have been laid during the last three decades, is becoming increasingly effective and viable. A great deal has been learned, and it is fortunate that many persons both in government and in the university community have remained responsibly involved throughout these years and are today able to bring to bear a considerable amount of wisdom and understanding. There is ground for optimism that within the partnership we may see growing leadership by the institutions of higher education.

Lynton K. Caldwell

The University-Government Relationship

By the middle of the 1960's, university-government relations in international programs have achieved a state of "dynamic equilibrium." This relationship appears to be more congenial to the interests of the respective parties than anything that prevailed during the preceding decade and a half of "partnership" in programs overseas. If this relationship proves viable and amenable to the inevitable adaptations that new circumstances require, one may conclude that the parties have indeed learned from experience.

During the years of university-government contention over the terms and administration of overseas contracts, there was reason to doubt that any rapprochement satisfactory to the parties and consistent with program objectives would emerge. Influential minorities, both bureaucratic and academic, argued that the objectives of government and of universities were fundamentally dissimilar and that the universities could not serve the purposes of government overseas without loss of autonomy and integrity. The advent of the Gardner report [1] and of David Bell as AID administrator marked the emergence of a new, flexible, and experience-based effort to achieve a workable relationship between government and university. Although it would be protesting too much to declare that the improved relationship is completely satisfactory to the parties, it is clear that in principle each has

[1] John W. Gardner, *AID and the Universities,* Report from Education and World Affairs in Cooperation with the Agency for International Development (New York: Education and World Affairs, 1964).

arrived at a more reasonable and realistic understanding than before of what partnership implies and requires.

Both the government and the universities are today better able to weigh the factors involved in entering upon a contractual relationship than were either a decade ago. This is a substantial accomplishment and one achieved only through considerable turmoil and travail. It required, on both sides, a clarification of government and university perspectives. Government and university personnel today are far closer to a common concept of the international assistance task than they were in 1950 or 1960. The basic commitments of the two parties are still different but, with respect to their joint efforts, there has been a convergence of policy. For the most part AID officials have come to understand that a university is not just another purveyor of commodities and that it must be met halfway with adequate appreciation for its special circumstances and problems if it is to be effectively utilized overseas. Correspondingly, in the universities there is less disposition than formerly to confuse government contracts with foundation grants. Universities entering into contractual relationships with government today have no excuse for failing to understand the additional commitment that this association will require of them. Moreover, several aspects of the new relationship have been institutionalized in ways that will make for stability and continuity in the new patterns of association.

A Problem of Concepts

The troubled history of university-government relationships in overseas programs was in large measure a consequence of confusion in concepts. It was not that academic and bureaucratic concepts of the overseas task were necessarily in conflict. They *were* occasionally in conflict, but more often they were merely different. These differences might have been, and sometimes were, transcended or modified through the mediation of perceptive individuals on either side. Very often, however, conceptual differences led the parties into conflicting assumptions regarding the task to be accomplished and the conditions necessary for its accomplishment. In consequence a deep and pervasive hostility toward university contractors developed among many AID officials.[2] This dislike was reciprocated by those academic personnel who, unaccustomed to conditions of government employment, saw their responsibilities as extending solely to their academic employer and profession.

These tensions handicapped communication between the universities and the government. Candor became hazardous when seized upon by either adversary as a weapon in gamemanship to be turned against the candid opponent. Failure to find a way to achieve and maintain common concepts of the overseas task led to extensive by-passing of discourse in contract negotiations, in administration, and especially in evaluation or termination phases of the relationship. Difficulties grew because at the outset neither of the parties had a clear concept of what joint efforts would entail. As the respective concepts crystalized and clarified through experience, they also often tended to diverge. Throughout the 1950's efforts to clarify these concepts often had the effect of sharpening conflicts.

Any valid generalization regarding university and government concepts of the overseas assistance task should imply inevitable exceptions on both sides. But the main tendencies in approach to the assistance task are clear.

The government official, in the main, conceived the task as a technical operation susceptible to definite programming, budgeting, and timing. Considerable importance has been attached to bureaucratic procedures, to clearance, semiannual reports, and program review. Even greater importance has been attached to the avoidance of possible embarrassment or criticism resulting from "irresponsible" action on the part of university contract personnel. The more insecure the AID official (in an agency

[2] Throughout this paper, except when specific reference is necessary, AID and AID officials refers not only to the Agency for International Development but to its predecessor agencies, e.g., TCA, MSA, FOA, and ICA. The early history of the United States foreign aid organization and effort was described by Rollin S. Atwood, "The United States Point Four Program—A Bilateral Approach," in *Partnership for Progress: International Technical Cooperation,* edited by Richard W. Gable, *The Annals of the American Academy of Political and Social Science,* CCCXXIII (May 1959), 33-39.

in which insecurity has been endemic), the more apprehensive he was likely to be regarding contract performance. In consequence, "riding herd" on contracts often seemed to have been the agency concept of its normal functional relationship to the contracting universities.

Contrasting the priority accorded long-range education in the aid programs of European nations with American impatient insistence on direct action, a leading analyst of international development efforts observed: "In contrast to the more gradualist approach of the Europeans and their absence of any very compelling sense of urgency, the United States seems preoccupied with impact projects and self-imposed deadlines that are useful in mobilizing resources but carry the seeds of subsequent disappointment."[3] This search for quick results was spurred by an uncomprehending Congress, public, and press. The result was to encourage rapid and quixotic shifts of AID policy with the manifest concern of overseas mission officers to "phase-out" existing contracts as scheduled and then move on to new efforts in pursuit of the chimera of quick and evident results. Long-range educational efforts were obviously incompatible with this set of mind.

The university personnel, in the main, conceived their task in long-range developmental terms. Not only have they characteristically doubted that educational growth in cross-cultural situations could be rigidly programmed, but they have been especially sensitive to decisions made by government officials regarding their work. The state universities have traditionally been concerned with maintaining independence from policy interference on the part of state school administrators, fiscal officers, and legislators. The academic community generally has a conditioned-reflex or built-in resistance to interpositions from the non-academic world. Thus the AID official, who wishes to review proposed publications of university contract staff in the interest of American foreign policy and agency responsibility, may find his intentions regarded from the academic perspective as censorship, witch-hunting, and thought-control. The concept of academic freedom,

[3] Robert E. Asher, "How to Succeed in Foreign Aid without Really Trying," *Public Policy*, XIII (Cambridge: Harvard University Press, 1964), 131.

from the vantage point of public office, may resemble a calculated anarchy; but when threatened, university faculties of all political persuasions invariably unite in its defense. Academic deans have learned to live with quasi-anarchy and to administer it so as to achieve at least a minimal essential of system and order in university affairs. But skill in manipulating the "guided democracy" of the university is acquired only by long exposure to, or immersion in, the academic environment. It requires a high order of intuitive endowment and a sensitivity to academic assumptions and ground rules "known" to university communities, but never fully spelled out in faculty handbooks, and not readily comprehended by "outsiders."

The universities were brought into the aid program with little appreciation of what the relationship with government entailed. Idealism on both sides has been further insulated from operational realities by the well-known tendency of higher government officials and university presidents to talk broad generalities, accentuate the positive, and leave routines and details to lower echelon personnel. As one moves down in the respective hierarchies of government and academia, innate institutional tendencies become accentuated. The petty bureaucrat is proverbially a stickler for rules and the assistant professor, more frequently than his seniors, pictures himself as a torch-bearer for freedom of thought.

These differences in perspective and in concept characteristically have complicated the course of contract relationships following negotiation. The honeymoon period of a contract is likely to be more harmonious than subsequent day-to-day relations amidst the difficulties and frustrations of cross-cultural assistance efforts. The attitude of higher level officials, amicable and accommodating at the outset, tends to harden and become more protective of institutional interests as these officials are required to decide upon issues arising from lower administrative levels. The very nature of the administrative process makes it difficult for an official to overrule his staff. Moreover, in the AID organization, subordinate staff easily "outlive" mission chiefs, who frequently lack experience in the field of foreign assistance. Thus those least sympathetic with the overseas role of universities have often been the most influential in shaping the policies of the United States overseas missions.

Mission directors abroad frequently have been appointed from private enterprise careers, innocent of previous experience with either government or university administration. Whatever their bias regarding government bureaucracy, these businessmen-mission directors often have become "captives" of their more knowledgeable subordinates, particularly the mission economic and legal staff. Prior experience with procurement, accounting, and production schedules, for example, makes it easier for them to relate to the more routinized and quantitative aspects of public administration. The businessman's proverbial impatience with theory, and his characteristic suspicion of "professors" further complicates relations with the universities. The mission director is also constrained by his official position to maintain cordial relations with his host country officials whom academic contract staff often viewed as stupid, corrupt, and anti-democratic. A symbolic example illustrates contrasting perspectives: While the mission director played golf with ministers and generals, university contract staff drank beer with local "intellectuals" and labor leaders. In consequence each side, government and university, could develop a very different perspective on what the assistance effort required.

Incompatible Commitments

Even if concepts and perspectives had been essentially the same, government and the universities would nevertheless have encountered operational difficulties growing out of fundamental institutional commitments.

The AID administrators have not been able properly or easily to evade the political premise of the American "foreign aid" effort. The aid program has been an altruistic effort, but it has also been an instrument of American foreign and military policy. Much of it has been unpopular with the Congress and the country, reluctantly supported because of cold war considerations. A percentage of "old-hands" in the Department of State saw the technical assistance program, particularly in its university contract phase, as mischievous. More than one American ambassador voiced apprehension at the coteries of unofficial amateur academic ambassadors running around host countries without hindrance or let. In one Asian country the ambassador saw aid to education and public administration as impinging on areas too sensitive for risk. Military and monetary assistance were, in his judgment, the prudent limits of "foreign aid." Another ambassador, following a policy of appeasing a capricious and exploitive host country dictator, lectured the president of a contracting university on the necessity of his academic staff accommodating themselves to the "hardships" of the country. In fact, the university personnel in this instance had an exemplary record of adaptation to local conditions and had attempted to protect their on-the-job effectiveness from attrition in a bureaucratic feud between two host country agencies.

In the interests of foreign policy, AID officials understandably have preferred short-term and narrowly defined arrangements to long-term guarantees. Universities conversely, conceiving their task as long-range in character, have sought long-term government commitment to see the effort through. In brief, the institutional position of the government argued for close supervision of university contract activities and minimal commitment to financial and policy support. On the other hand, the institutional university position argued for firm and continuing financial and policy support by government and minimal interference in matters of program execution. For example, mission staff tended to view contract renewal as a tactical weapon with which to exact concessions or reforms from host governments. But while negotiators wrangled, the university was left in a state of suspension, unable to plan for continuation of its contract efforts and uncertain of the consequences of termination.

On their side, the universities had a commitment to the advancement of learning that government officials were slow to acknowledge in the context of overseas contracts. Contention often developed over the role of "research" in overseas contracts.

To the university faculty member, one of the most attractive inducements to overseas service was research opportunity. That this opportunity could seldom be offered to prospective overseas staff narrowed considerably the field of academic recruitment. Many university faculty members, including many of the more prestigious, were unwilling to abandon research interests at home for two years of teaching and public service in some remote and backward area abroad. Their reluctance was usually directly proportionate to the state of development in the host country. In countries needing aid most, teaching was likely to be at a rudimentary level. Service activities, low priority among academic values at home, could hardly be expected to enjoy greater reputation in an "underdeveloped" country.

Several consequences followed from the absence of research opportunity in most of the earlier overseas contract programs. One of these was that host countries often failed to receive the distinguished scholars that they had somehow been led to expect would come to them on contract assignments. Instead of big-name scholars with distinguished research reputations, the contract staff was characteristically made up of younger, less-known academics, often without pronounced research interests. Mission personnel were also sometimes disappointed in the caliber of contract staff, having shared certain of the host country misconceptions. Their disappointments were not always justified. A younger and less specialized contract team was often better prepared to render the service required than would have a comparable number of distinguished service professors. But status consciousness among host country and AID officials too often led to downgrading the reputation of the contract to the hierarchical level of its staff.

The reputation of the contracts on university home campuses was also prejudiced in some instances by the failure to include a research component. While faculty members serving abroad often experienced notable personal growth and satisfaction, some grew in professional stature, and some contract assignments led to accelerated academic or professional advancement; for others overseas service proved a dead-end road. It is doubtful, however, that many of these would have fared better had they remained at home. Some of these were without strong commitments to research and without clearly developed skills in teaching. Others, however, possessed skills in cross-cultural communication and mid-career development work that found more opportunity abroad than in universities at home.

From the university viewpoint, research was important in the contract programs in two respects: *first* and most obviously, to maximize the opportunities that the contract afforded to the university; *second,* as a foundation for the overseas program itself. At the outset both government and the universities were overly optimistic about the adequacy of academic resources for the overseas tasks, but it rapidly became evident that most academic personnel had much to learn before they could be fully effective in most of the countries in which they were asked to serve. Not only were American academics frequently unable to handle indigenous languages overseas, but little was actually known about the psychology, value structure, politics, and educational practices of the host countries. Thus many faculty members viewed government contract programs that failed to provide for preparatory research and academic development as methodologically unsound.

Development of their faculty and informational resources was perceived by universities as closely related to contract research and orientation. They saw the necessity for AID support in tooling-up to do the overseas job, whereas the AID official tended to view the involvement of the university as procurement of a service already available on the market. To the AID official who expected to buy educational services the way one bought tractors, academic insistence on research and development was evidence of four-flushing or freeloading on the part of the universities. More than a decade was required to bring government officials to the realization that a legitimate part of the aid effort must include building up academic resources for overseas assistance. The AID official was committed to spend aid funds abroad; developing the facilities and libraries of American universities at home did not seem a legitimate use of contract funds. Government and university representatives wrangled for years over whether (or how much) language training and orientation were chargeable as contract expenses.

In brief, the basic institutional commitments of the government and the universities complicated their working relationships. Each party within the terms of his own logic could feel his position to be right. But there were certain overriding necessities in the process of cross-cultural cooperation that gradually forced a convergence of viewpoint. It became increasingly evident with the accumulation of experience that commitment to the task of overseas assistance would have to modify traditional institutional commitments on both sides if the university-government relationship was to continue.

The Process of Policy Convergence

Experientia docet (experience teaches), observed the historian Tacitus. And indeed experience has been the school in which government and the universities have learned the relationships that have proved most fruitful in overseas contract programs. No adequate or tested theory was available for guidance in 1951 at the outset of university-government contract relationship in "foreign aid."[4] Experience very soon revealed important differences in concept and commitment between the parties.[5] These differences could seldom be resolved between the United States government and specific contracting universities. The partners were far from equal and, in the event of disagreement, the government always had recourse to unilateral action. Under the early phase of the aid program directed by Henry G. Bennett (who had been president of Oklahoma State University) and Harold Stassen who became director of the unified aid program in 1953, enthusiasm

[4] For the details of university-government relationships in the initiation and early years of overseas contract programs, see "The University and Technical Assistance Abroad" in Edward W. Weidner, *The World Role of Universities* (New York: McGraw-Hill Book Company, 1962), pp. 153-172.

[5] Many of the differences and difficulties were described by Henry Reining, Jr., "The Government Contract as an Administrative Device" in *Partnership for Progress*, pp. 68-79.

for university overseas contracts was sustained, at least at top AID levels. After 1954 however, Agriculture and other subject-matter agencies of the federal government no longer played a direct or important role in technical assistance as they had at first. A new and less sympathetic AID director and the increasing influence of the legal and fiscal staff of the aid agency accompanied a steady deterioration of university-government relationships. It became evident that concerted action among the universities would be necessary to establish their position in reaction to the government and to obtain governmental acquiescence in matters on which they felt unable to compromise.

Through efforts of the American Council on Education and the (then) Association of Land-Grant Colleges and Universities, machinery was developed to negotiate points of difference with AID administrators and to arrive at a mutually acceptable understanding of appropriate relationships. The Committee (and Office) on Institutional Projects Abroad, established by the American Council on Education in September of 1954, became the principal forum in which the principles and details governing contract relationships were worked out. In a report on its first year of operations, the Committee summarized its responsibilities as: "(1) a service to assist in contract negotiations and administration, and in the operation of the program; (2) a focus of identification for major problems of policy, planning and development; and (3) a source of informed counsel to all concerned."[6]

As might be expected the day-to-day attention of the Committee tended to focus on operating details of the relationships rather than on the principles by which the university-government relationship should be defined and be governed. This was a natural stage in the evolution of the relationships. Specific points of friction and misunderstanding needed to be somehow resolved long before cumulating experience had indicated what the relationship must be in principle in order to be effective. Larger aspects of the university-government relationship were explored at conferences convened by the Committee at East Lansing (1955),

[6] Report on First Year of Operation (August 1955), p. 1.

Washington (1956), Denver (1957), and again in Washington (1958, 1959, 1960).

Related in purpose were meetings of university contract coordinators sometimes with and sometimes without AID officials. Among these meetings were those held at Indiana University in 1958 and at Colorado State University in 1963. The agendas at these gatherings understandably tended to focus on grievances. These occasions were also used, however, by AID officials to interpret and clarify agency policy for the coordinators.

Beyond the necessary attention to procedural and policy matters, a continuing objective of the American Council on Education and of the Committee on Institutional Projects Abroad was to establish in principle a basis upon which specific controversies could be resolved. To this end the Committee, in April 1955, circulated a policy statement among universities entitled "The Participation of American Colleges and Universities in Technical Cooperation Programs Abroad." The "operating principles and assumptions" set forth by the Committee reflected an academic consensus, but unfortunately could be given a latitude of interpretation so wide as to afford little guidance in actual university-government relationships.

In paraphrase, the statement argued that (1) university assistance in the aid program should be sought in education and research (but were the typical AID efforts in institution-building, training and demonstration "education" or "research"?); (2) government-university contract relationships should be on a no profit-no loss basis (but what constitutes proper cost accounting?); (3) American faculty members abroad must adapt to local customs and situations as well as to the requirements of public policy, (but who decides what patterns of collaboration with host country nationals are consistent with American foreign policy?); (4) once a contract is established, full *professional-technical* responsibility and authority should rest with the contracting university (but who determines what is a *professional-technical* matter, and what happens when academic and political judgments contradict?); and (5) universities should make available faculty of highest caliber "despite the pressures of regular programs" and should build the overseas effort into the normal structure of the university (but how are these highest caliber faculty members to be persuaded to serve? And how much effort can universities realistically be expected to expend on programs that are not perceived as "regular"?). In short, these principles stated the university viewpoint, but did not really provide a common ground upon which government and the universities could negotiate their differences.

During 1955 the irritations and frustrations of the contracting universities continued to grow. On August 16 the Office of Institutional Projects Abroad (which served the Committee) circulated among the 43 contract institutions a questionnaire which was the basis for "A Summary of Institutional Views on the University Contract Program," a background paper for the Conference on University Projects Abroad held November 17-18 at Michigan State University. This paper detailed a large number of complaints against government handling of university contracts. The contractors objected particularly to: "(1) cross-cutting standard university administrative practices, (2) constant checks and amendments, (3) lack of provision for contingencies, (4) multiplicity of forms, and (5) 'purposefully imprecise' definitions." Relations with the aid organization (then International Cooperation Administration) were described as "unduly time-consuming, arbitrary, and confusing."

Commenting on the report and on the worsening state of government-university relationships, President John A. Hannah of Michigan State University told the 1955 Conference on University Contracts Abroad that the time had come "to investigate objectively with Mr. Dulles, Mr. Hollister [AID administrator], and the White House, if necessary, to determine what their feelings are. . . . I don't know Mr. Hollister," he added, "but I haven't seen anything he has said or written that indicates he has any awareness at all of this university program."[7]

---

[7] Richard A. Humphrey (ed.), *University Projects Abroad*, Papers Presented at the Conference on University Contracts Abroad, Michigan State University, Lansing, November 17-18, 1955 (Washington: American Council on Education, 1956), p. 54.

Although high-placed AID officials assured the universities of their importance in government overseas efforts, relationships did not improve. Then, in a May 25 commencement address at Baylor University, President Eisenhower made a strong plea for the involvement of American universities in the development of the new nations. Reaction among universities was understandably cautious. Was the President oblivious to circumstances prevailing in his own administration? Some critics saw in the Baylor address further indication of the President's highly personalized view of public affairs—combining a realistic appraisal of need with an unrealistic assessment of means. His remarks clearly endorsed higher education as a major instrument of American foreign policy but referred responsibility for this development to private institutions and foundations. These views added little clarity to the already confused relations of universities and government.

On June 19, 1956, the American Council on Education convened a joint meeting of its Commission on Education and International Affairs and the Committee on Institutional Projects Abroad to consider the implications of the President's address. Was the President to be taken seriously? The joint meeting found that: "Although there appeared to be differing reactions among institutions of higher education in different parts of the country, the discussion disclosed no evidence that the President's proposals invoked strong enthusiasm among the educational fraternity." Nevertheless, "it was agreed that, whatever the President's intentions may have been, the fact of the Baylor Proposal had to be taken into serious account."[8]

An outcome of the June 19 meeting was appointment of a special joint committee under the chairmanship of Herman B Wells, president of Indiana University, to prepare (among other tasks) a policy statement on government-university relationships in international affairs. A preliminary draft of a general policy statement and progress report on the Work of the Special Joint Committee were discussed by the Commission and Committee on

[8] Minutes of Joint Meeting, p. 1.

November 9, 1956. The report called for partnership between higher education and government "on a basis of equality with each assuming leadership in areas of their special competence," and urged "greater coordination among government and private programs." It also recommended establishing "a central source of information on existing programs, on resources for expansion of activities, and on overseas needs and potential cooperation."

The Council also initiated a survey of its membership to ascertain the "views of American educators on policies that should govern their work in this field." The report on the results of this survey, published April 17, 1957, under the title *International Activities of American Colleges and Universities,* indicated that the academic community believed that: (1) "The Government does not understand the problems our institutions face in conducting international educational programs," and "conversely, the institutions do not understand Government policies and procedures, nor do many institutions know what opportunities for service exist;" (2) American higher education should insist on greater participation in the development of policies and programs for government financed activities which are conducted at the university level; and (3) "that the broad purpose of international educational activities is to *educate* so as to bring about understanding and exchange of ideas across national boundaries."[9]

Concurrently, the actual state of government-university contract relationships continued to worsen. The lowest and perhaps most critical point in the relationship was reached late in November 1956, when university dissatisfaction with evidences of apparent official hostility in the then International Cooperation Administration grew so intense that representatives of the then American Association of Land-Grant Colleges and Universities were ready to lay their case directly before President Dwight D. Eisenhower at the White House. The Association, comprising 71 institutions and representing real political power served warning on the International Cooperation Administration that it could expect withdrawal of many institutions from the aid program

[9] p. 3. (The report was reprinted from the October 1957 issue of *The Educational Record* published by the American Council on Education.)

because of the "lack of major concern for and support of institutional contracts abroad at top ICA administrative levels."[10] In an "eleventh hour" appearance before a conference of university representatives in Washington, ICA director John B. Hollister affirmed the government's friendly feeling toward the universities and assured the gathering that the presumed official hostility was all a misunderstanding.

The confrontation with John Hollister did indeed mark an upturning of university-government relationships. In what had approached a test of political strength, the combined power of the universities, particularly of the great land-grant and state universities, had been manifest. Without question there were ICA officials who would have welcomed termination of all university contract relationships. Their motives ranged from those of certain higher echelon appointees to whom all college professors were unreliable, to lower level careerists who saw in contract personnel a displacement of government jobs, and whose advancement would be furthered by acquiring a number of administrative subordinates but who would never be rewarded merely for doing a good job of expediting contract programs. If there had been thought of eliminating university participation in the overseas aid program, it did not appear to have received serious consideration after the Hollister confrontation.

Although the universities had won a victory of sorts, it was a victory of little substance—a moral victory rather than an establishment of a new relationship. Many university representatives wished to have an office of university relations established in the AID agency headed by someone who understood university concepts and commitments. But this development was to be postponed for a number of years. Not until 1965 did AID establish an office corresponding to this viewpoint, and even then it did not possess the powers that its early advocates desired. In the interim, the AID contract office became the principal point of agency-university contact. But the nature of that office determined

---

[10] Press Release No. 46, November 14, 1956 (Convention Press Room, Willard Hotel, Washington). As of November 11, 1964, the organization has been renamed the National Association of State Universities and Land-Grant Colleges.

the nature of the way in which relationships were conceptualized and implemented. Contract office staff were primarily concerned with legal and fiscal relationships. A broader framework of relationship was assumed to exist, but was nowhere made explicit. In point of fact, an agreed concept of such a normative relationship did not exist.

In 1957, the American Council on Education sponsored negotiations between the government and the universities which led to a so-called "standard" contract. Characteristically, these negotiations were carried on between business officers of the universities and the legal staff of the contract office. In 1959 a special subcommittee of the Committee on Institutional Projects Abroad was established to assume continuing responsibilities for negotiating university contract problems with the AID organization. The negotiators were, for the most part, well equipped to deal with contract detail, but were not in position to consider the broader philosophical and institutional issues implicit in the university-government relationship. But by clearing away the more troublesome points of difference at operative levels the way was opened for subsequent consideration of the large issues. These found expression in the report of John Gardner, President of the Carnegie Foundation, submitted to AID administrator David Bell on March 2, 1964.

The Gardner report was, in fact, the culmination of a decade and a half of thought and experience on university-government relationships in the broader and more basic sense. In the background of the report were developments in American higher education that assisted the universities in clarifying and strengthening their position regarding the university-government relationship. A brief look at the more influential of these developments is a logical prelude to examination of the Gardner report.

Early in the 1960's the big foundations began to put sizeable grants of money into research on developing countries. "Development" became the talisman by which financial assistance for overseas and international cross-cultural research could be obtained. For example, the Comparative Administration Group of the American Society for Public Administration received an initial grant of a quarter of a million dollars from the Ford Foundation for studies designed to enlarge understanding of the development process. Foundation support was made available to universities for Asian, African, and Latin American studies. To some extent these grants provided research opportunities that complemented or paralleled contract activities and thus made the overseas government contract programs more attractive to university faculties.

Confronted by the rising tide of militant and anti-Western nationalism throughout large areas of the world, and apparent failures in countries where the nation had made heavy investment in aid expenditures, the Departments of State and Defense sought assistance from the universities and research organizations in probing the roots of political behavior. Studies undertaken by the Brookings Institution and the RAND Corporation added to the accumulating evidence regarding the complexities and uncertainties of the process of national development. Following its establishment in October 1957, the Society for International Development had begun to provide a highly relevant forum for discussion of the problems encountered in cross-cultural technical assistance and one in which university people, government officials, and business leaders intermixed.

Apart from the work of the committees of the American Council on Education, perhaps the most direct influence on converging perspectives in government and universities was a number of high-level studies on international affairs undertaken by committees of distinguished citizens with foundation support in the late 1950's or early 60's. Among these, the study most directly bearing on the university-government relationship was that of the Committee on the University and World Affairs, chaired by J. L. Morrill, recently retired president of the University of Minnesota, and including prominent business and foundation executives and public officials.[11] The report of the Committee, issued in December

[11] Among a larger number of relevant studies and reports were: National Planning Association, Special Committee on Technical Cooperation, *The Role of Universities in Technical Cooperation* (Washington: National Planning Association, 1955), one of the earliest studies; American Assembly, *Cultural Affairs and Foreign Relations,* edited by Robert Blum (Englewood Cliffs, N.J.: Prentice-Hall, 1963);

1960, reinforced the position taken by the universities in relation to the aid program. With specific reference to the International Cooperation Administration, the report declared:

> ICA should move more rapidly toward increased emphasis on educational development. The university contract is an effective instrument to marshal the resources of the universities for programs of educational assistance. This contract relationship, however, can be improved to provide the autonomy and flexibility appropriate to the university's participation with government in a cooperative undertaking. Universities should be brought in at an earlier stage of planning. Greater care should be exercised in choosing overseas projects appropriate for university contracts and in finding the appropriate university for a particular overseas contract or participant training assignment. The contract or the participant training agreement should serve also to build the university's own resources by improving its competence in teaching and research. Universities selected need to have an assurance of continuity in the ICA program itself which is essential to permit the university to make necessary long-term commitments for staff and facilities and which cannot be derived solely from lengthening particular contracts. Lastly, financial and accounting provisions in the contract arrangements should be further simplified.[12]

Here, in essence, was a statement of the relationship with the government that the universities sought. To these scholarly and professional efforts must be added the imponderable influence of critical journalism. Polemical fiction, such as *The Ugly American* (1958), undercut tradition bound and bureaucratic postures of State Department and AID officials. It seems very probable that fictional and nonfictional exposés of the gaucheries and miscalculations of aid efforts hastened the willingness of officials to give more considered attention to a better deployment of the nation's intellectual resources in the AID program.

United States Advisory Commission on International and Cultural Affairs, *A Beacon of Hope: The Exchange of Persons Program* (Washington: Government Printing Office, 1963) ; *The College and World Affairs,* A Report by the Committee on the College and World Affairs, John W. Nason, chairman (New York: The Hazen Foundation, 1964).

[12] *The University and World Affairs,* A Report by the Committee on the University and World Affairs, J. L. Morrill, chairman (New York: The Ford Foundation, 1960), p. 53.

Thus the groundwork was laid for the Gardner report prior to its publication. In the light of experience, scholarly research, aid scandals and polemics, the report seemed thoroughly reasonable and its recommendations overdue. Experience had indeed been a teacher—how convincing was, to some extent, a matter of opinion. In a very real sense the foreign aid task and environment had determined the character of the relationship between the universities and government. The need for country orientation, language training, and program flexibility long emphasized by universities had been demonstrated by events; and government resistance to building up resources for the overseas task had given way to a recognition that development of the means to achieve national policy objectives was a necessary part of the total effort.

The Gardner Report

In July 1963, AID administrator David E. Bell asked John W. Gardner (then president of the Carnegie Corporation of New York) "to organize a task force on AID and the universities, to examine carefully the relationships of the Agency with the universities, and to make such recommendations as he saw fit."[18] Assisted by the newly organized Education and World Affairs and by the American Council on Education, a committee of government and university representatives contributed to a synthesis and summation of what was widely perceived to be the appropriate government-university relationship in international programs. Contributory to the drafting of the report, the substance of the university-government relationship was discussed in the autumn of 1963 at a series of regional conferences sponsored by Education and World Affairs.

The report at the outset recognized that the AID-university relationship had been characterized by conflict and misunderstanding and that the most persistent irritants in the relationship had grown out of contract administration. But the report also observed that: "Many problems in contract administration do not

[18] Gardner, *AID and the Universities*, p. ix.

stem from the contracting process and device but from broader
aspects of the relationships: confused definition of appropriate
roles and purposes, incomplete commitment of host country
leaders, short-run view of the aid program, budgetary and organization difficulties of the agency, and so on."[14] The basic requisite
for a fruitful relationship was identified as "the spirit and understanding prevailing at the outset. Both parties must achieve a
relatively thorough understanding of what is to be done and of
the nature of the commitment each is making."[15] How was this
understanding to be achieved?

The report recognized that a perfect identity of interests and
commitments was not attainable. But it identified certain conditions that could lead to a much closer rapprochement and more
effective working relationships. These were: (1) higher professional quality among AID career personnel—"first-class people
capable of dealing with outside individuals and institutions on
terms of professional equality;" (2) a government-university
relationship "defined in such a way as to preserve to each party
independence of action in those functions that it must perform
unimpeded;" (3) a relationship in which "each party can not only
perform at its best but can gain added strength from its participation."[16]

The Gardner report did not define the university-government
relationship in any single comprehensive statement. The essential elements of the relationship required for effective collaboration were nevertheless clearly discernible in the text of the report.
To state these elements incisively it is therefore necessary to
paraphrase the report, to draw together the substance of these
elements from the several sections of the report in which they
appear.

The components of an effective university-government relationship as conceived by the Gardner report were four.

1. The proper role of the university (with minor exceptions) is "the achievement of long-term purposes: educational
growth and human resource development, the advancement of

[14] *Ibid.*, p. 24.   [15] *Ibid.*   [16] *Ibid.*, p. 2.

knowledge, and the application of knowledge to basic problems."[17]

This precept indicates the unsuitability of universities for most short-term piecemeal assignments and for contracts not basically educational in character. The long-term and complex character of programs suitable for university involvement not only indicates the need for early involvement of the university in the planning phase of programs, but also affords justification for government investment in the long-term growth of university potential in the fields relating to international service.

2. The university is an indispensable national resource in the aid effort and the government, as it draws upon it, "must build strength back into the resource for future use."[18]

This viewpoint argues for spending part of the available foreign aid funds to improve our future capacity rather than to live off our intellectual capital. It argues for the legitimacy of aid expenditures to strengthen university faculties and library resources for the overseas aid task and it clearly indicates the inclusion of research as a normal part of university contract activity.

3. The nature of the universities' unique role in international technical assistance, the nature of the university as an organization, and the long-term character of the educational and developmental task indicate the need for operational flexibility in the university-government relationship.[19]

The Gardner report recognized the great difficulty of defining in the abstract the degree of autonomy to be enjoyed by the university in the field. "The nearest we can come to such a formula," the report declared, "is the assertion that universities functioning overseas should enjoy the maximum *reasonable* degree of autonomy."[20] The areas in which government-university relations could be fruitful were those in which a high degree of operational flexibility could be accorded to responsi-

[17] *Ibid.*, p. 7.   [18] *Ibid.*, p. 11.
[19] *Ibid.*, cf. pp. 7-9, 25-26.   [20] *Ibid.*, p. 8.

ble universities. Policy areas requiring close foreign policy or mission supervision were not suitable for university involvement.

4. The university cannot enter into effective partnership with the government unless the whole university is involved. This does not necessarily imply centralized university administration of all overseas contracts but does imply that the "full weight and dignity" of each institution is behind any contract it accepts.

"When a university accepts a contract it should take it seriously, accept full responsibility, and put the whole institution behind the contract." [21] The chances of irresponsible behavior are greatly increased where the overseas activities are not accepted as *"an integral part of university life and work."*[22] A major cause of government-university friction has been the contract which a university has permitted individual faculty members or departments to negotiate with the government without any feeling of responsibility for the program on the part of the university as a whole. When the inevitable rough periods in contract operations arise, the university administration has sometimes been unjustifiably irritated with both its faculty and the government. Good relationships require clear and realistic appraisals of mutual responsibilities at the outset.

The observations contained in the Gardner report represent a convergence of viewpoints to which most university administrators and government officials would now subscribe. To recapitulate the relationship in summary form, the university-government relationship in assistance programs overseas should:

1. Be of a long-term educational character;

2. Strengthen and enlarge university resources for present and future aid tasks;

[21] *Ibid.,* p. 9.   [22] *Ibid.,* p. 10.

3. Be implemented in substantive areas and for purposes consistent with maximum university autonomy and operational flexibility; and

4. Be confined to efforts in which the university will wholeheartedly commit the requisite attention and resources.

By implication, contracts and programs inconsistent with these four criteria are not suitable for university-government relationships. Simple and apparent as these points appear to be in 1966, they were very much less apparent in 1951. Experience was necessary to establish their validity and to provide criteria or benchmarks by which the meaning of these precepts could be interpreted in particular cases.

Institutionalizing the New Relationship

Following publication of the Gardner report, action began toward revision of the 1957 standard university contract. Revision of the contract was discussed at the International Rural Development Conference in Washington in July 1964, and at the Modernizing of Nations Conference in Detroit in September. After further preliminary discussions between AID and university representatives, joint government-university planning sessions were held by AID in Washington (in November 1964 and January 1965). Four regional conferences were then arranged to explain the revised contract to present contracting universities and to others who might be interested.

Changes in the new standard contract confirmed many of the detailed provisions that universities had sought.[23] Among these were authorization for orientation and language training for outgoing faculty and staff and their dependents, contract-related research, and reimbursement for services of graduate students. Other provisions of the new standard contract clarified, liberalized, and regularized salary provisions, audit and termination

[23] Cf. *Bulletin on International Education,* III (March 1965), 1-2.

provisions, conditions of overseas service, and the adjudication of disputes between AID and the universities. These changes in the standard contract for universities reflected a more nearly stabilized university-government relationship. AID officials have also stated their intention to continue to revise and refine the standard contract from time to time. In late 1966 the agency was already in the process of updating the 1965 standard contract to improve certain provisions.

Other steps to institutionalize the convergent views of an effective university-government relationship were the appointment of a special assistant for university relations in the AID Office of Technical Cooperation and Research, the introduction by Senator McGovern of South Dakota of a bill (S.1212, February 19, 1965) to provide additional and continuing support for developing the capabilities of the universities for international services. Though the McGovern proposal was never enacted, the foreign aid legislation for 1966 authorized a special program of grants to universities to strengthen their potential for international service. The resulting so-called university grants program, though modest in scale and only now in the formative stages, will provide long-range support for institutional development in this area. Another step was the negotiation of agreements with organized groups of universities for special research studies. One of these was negotiated with the Midwest Committee on Institutional Cooperation (comprising the universities of Chicago, Illinois, Indiana, Iowa, Michigan, Michigan State, Minnesota, Northwestern, Ohio State, Purdue, and Wisconsin) for the purpose of analyzing the effectiveness of agricultural and rural development agricultural programs. A second was negotiated with the Inter-University Research Program in Institution-Building (the universities of Pittsburgh, Indiana, Michigan, and Syracuse) to study organizations and techniques for promoting the development process.

Also, several kinds of conferences have been held and committees created to improve communication and coordination between AID and the universities and among the universities themselves. Some of these have been held abroad; some in the

United States. Some have been concerned with area problems, or country problems; some with problems in one field or discipline. In addition to these activities addressed to specific operational problems in various areas of the world, AID established a high-level committee to consider on a regular basis the broad problems affecting the government-university relationship. The advisory committee on AID-university relations, composed primarily of university presidents and heads of educational associations, has met semiannually since late 1965 to counsel AID on such concerns as publication policy and criteria for the selection of university contractors. The agency is having a special study made in an attempt to develop guidelines for selection criteria.

The most important factor in the improved relationship, however, could not be institutionalized but was necessary in order to make all other changes work as intended. This was the quality of administrative personnel. Both the government and the universities had developed an appreciation of the personnel aspect of their relationships upon which effective cooperation depended. The Gardner report saw this personnel problem as vitally important in the AID agency, observing that: "(1) there must be close and continuous teamwork between the contract office and AID professional persons concerned with the contract. The importance of such teamwork can hardly be overestimated. (2) AID contract specialists handling university contracts should be individuals who have had experience in such dealings with the universities."[24] In the field, the Gardner report concluded that "the solution is less likely to come from formal attempts to define the relationship than from (a) a systematic attempt to staff AID field missions with men of high professional caliber, well-equipped by background and training to deal with the universities, and (b) a similar attempt by universities to ensure that senior members of field parties be men of proven judgment and stability as well as professional competence."[25]

The institutionalizing of a relationship implies, at the least,

[24] Gardner, *AID and the Universities*, p. 25.
[25] *Ibid.*, p. 9.

tacit agreement among the parties regarding their mutual obligations. A relationship may be said to be institutionalized when the concepts and practices indispensable to it have become sufficiently clear, firm, and continuing to afford a set of assumptions on which the parties to the relationship may rely. The process of institutionalizing a relationship occurs through the resolution of innumerable issues, many relatively insignificant, but collectively adding up to a trend. The process of convergence whereby the university-government relationship in overseas programs reached its present state of relative stability has been such a tendentious chain of events. An important element in this sequence, however, has been perceptive and articulate leadership at the critical points in time.

The initiation of a university-government relationship in overseas programs through the contract device was possible because of imaginative and persuasive leadership by the early AID directors and university presidents. University participation in the AID program in some form may have been inevitable. But it was *not* inevitable that the universities be involved collectively or as institutions. The government might have drawn upon higher education to meet its personnel needs abroad in a manner comparable to wartime service. But for the idealism of men who, in the right place and at the right time, saw the great potential of the university-government relationship, a magnificent possibility might have been lost. Had this leadership focused primarily on the difficulties and dissentions inherent in the relationship, the experiment might never have been attempted.

The trying years between 1954 and 1963 would have been difficult regardless of leadership. Yet inadequacies and failures on both sides did not destroy the vision of a university-government relationship that was fundamentally sound in concept. The process of learning how to implement the relationship—to translate vision into reality—went forward. A critical point was reached in 1962-63 when accumulated experience needed to be synthesized into a formulation more positive and realistic than the very general objectives with which the relationship began. At this juncture the university-government relationship was fortunate in a leadership that was exceptionally well qualified to consolidate the efforts of a decade and a half.

David E. Bell brought to the direction of the AID program in 1963 a personal understanding of government and university viewpoints and responsibilities. As Director of the Bureau of the Budget and principal author of the *Report to the President on Government Contracting for Research and Development,* [26] he had observed the problems of government contractual relationships with educational institutions in a context that was different from but not unrelated to the government-university relationship in "foreign aid." One of his early acts as AID director was to ask for the study on AID-university relationships that resulted in the Gardner report. Moreover, he became an effective interpreter of the report, performing the catalytic function that was necessary to confirm the relationship that events had combined to produce.

In confirming the relationship that had been achieved, David Bell did not describe a task that was completed. Instead he emphasized the achievement of a relationship in which learning and creative change might procede with maximum benefit to the program, the parties, and the nation. Addressing a conference on the Gardner report sponsored by Education and World Affairs, he argued that the measure of effectiveness in the university-government relationship was the extent to which it enabled the partners to learn from success and failure and to improve performance:

> Here AID and the universities share a responsibility and an opportunity. If a system of evaluation is built into the contract, it ought to be possible not only to evaluate efforts as we go but to learn as we go. I believe this will require significant changes in the way AID approaches the university contracts and in the way many universities think of their responsibilities under the contract. [27]

The university-government relationship in overseas programs is thus a strand in the complex interwoven network of relation-

[26] U.S., 87th Congress, 2nd Session, Senate Document No. 94 (May 17, 1962).

[27] "The University's Contribution to the Developing Nations," *Higher Education,* XX (March 1964), 7.

ships through which the public programs of our times are developed and administered. In the world of the 1960's and beyond, the public tasks are too vast and too complex to be undertaken by traditional government in isolation from the other institutions of modern society. The building of new relationships and new patterns of cooperation within society is inherent in the evolution that is symbolized by the United Nations, space technology, and the population explosion. Within this larger evolutionary framework one may see in full perspective the ultimate significance of a viable university-government relationship in the worldwide process of human development.

Alvin Roseman

The University
and Its Field Mission

The relationships of the American university under an AID overseas technical assistance contract have certain resemblances to those in a marriage. In both cases the arrangement is sanctioned by a legal formality, but no juristic words can define the interdependent associations in which the university's personnel are involved. As is often true in a marital compact, some of the most significant participants are not signatories to the covenant.

AID has utilized the services of American universities for three broad categories of overseas work. In the first, and simplest, type the university makes surveys and studies for the AID country mission and serves as a technical consultant to the official United States agency. It has no responsibility for advice or assistance to the government or institutions of the host country but merely submits to the mission its findings and recommendations on the specific matters which it has been asked to examine. This is usually a short-term, non-repetitive arrangement under which the university staff is overseas for a temporary period, completes its work, and goes home.

A second relationship is one in which the university undertakes, on behalf of the aid mission, to provide technical advice to the host government in some field of program activity over a period of several years. Under this plan, the university furnishes a type of professional service which is ordinarily supplied by directly employed staff of the mission.

Under the third category the university engages, through AID and the foreign government, to assist an educational institution in the host country with the development of its teaching and research work in one or more professional or disciplinary fields. This relationship usually involves an initial contractual period of three years, subject to renewal.

The first arrangement is a transitory one and ordinarily does not present any special problem of mission-university relationship. However, from the viewpoint of the university itself there obviously is a question as to whether this function is appropriate to an educational institution, or whether the faculty members concerned should be serving as individuals without responsibility on the part of the home campus.

Under the second system, the university becomes an adjunct of the aid mission. Its staff, in effect, functions as part of the mission and performs the various professional and administrative tasks involved in programming and executing a sector of the American aid effort in the country. This plan usually brings the university personnel directly into the process of negotiation between the host government and the mission. While services to one or more local educational institutions may be included in the scope of the university's work, the American faculty's primary relationship is with the appropriate governmental ministry.

In these circumstances the university personnel are subject to about the same supervisory controls by the mission director and his principal staff members as are applied to senior technical advisers directly employed by the mission. Like other responsible professional employees, the university representatives expect the mission director to respect their professional judgments, but they are also subjected to day-to-day supervisory decisions on such matters as priorities, allocation of resources, and relationships with other aspects of the aid program or with other American governmental activities. Under this type of contract, the American faculty members usually occupy office space in the mission's headquarters, which tends to identify them in the eyes of the host country institutions as part of the official United States organization.

This arrangement similarly poses some question of propriety.

In undertaking this second type of activity the American institution usually is performing a function which can also be carried out by non-academic organizations. It cannot claim academic prerogatives when it is operating outside the field in which such privileges are pertinent. A university which regards extension work of a public service character as one of its major responsibilities may not cavil at assuming responsibility for providing economic assistance activities to a foreign government in fields in which its faculty has technical competence. Nor will it consider the administrative relationships involved within the mission as necessarily inappropriate for its faculty. On the other hand, many American universities would consider a relationship of this character as completely outside the legitimate role of an institution of higher education.

The third arrangement does not, in itself, raise questions of legitimacy for most American universities, since cooperation with educational institutions in other countries has long been a traditional academic activity. A few American institutions have decided that they will not enter into AID-financed contracts because they object to the statutory personnel security requirements or to the governmental fiscal controls. But most United States universities have found it possible to live with these contracts even if they consider some of their provisions unnecessarily rigid.

When the American university is engaged to assist in the development of an overseas institution of higher education, it is functioning in a field in which it can claim unique competence. Obviously there must be agreement between the university and AID concerning the objectives and scope of the contract, but the university can properly maintain that the aid mission is not qualified to supervise the professional work of its faculty, control their methods of operation, or evaluate the effectiveness of their effort.

Failure to distinguish between these types of relationships has led to difficulties between university groups and aid missions. If a university accepts the Queen's shilling for non-academic work, it must also accept non-academic supervision. On the other hand, if the university's task is one which only an educational institution can appropriately undertake, it has the right to claim relative autonomy within the general scope of the agreed task.

The AID Mission and the University Team

The work of the American university's representatives stationed abroad is the basic determinant of the success of the institution's overseas technical assistance contract. The supporting tasks on the home campus are also important, but it is in the field that the university has its closest and most intimate relationships with the other participants in the contractual arrangement. These usually include the USAID mission, the American embassy, the government of the cooperating country, and the host institution.

The university team's operations in the field are much different from those which most American faculty undertake at home. The members of the American university overseas group normally will do some teaching and research because of their own internal compulsions and because it is through their teaching that they secure acceptance by their foreign academic colleagues. However, they will devote a much greater proportion of their time to planning programs and curricula, developing teaching material, training future faculty, advising on organization, and other activities of a managerial character than would be their lot in the United States. Their basic task overseas is to supply technical assistance in educational planning and administration, a function which most American university faculty prefer to leave to their deans and administrative officers.

The members of the field party also are involved in channels of control quite different from those to which they are accustomed. They are, of course, employees of their own university and receive substantive and administrative supervision from the home campus. However, under the terms of the standard AID university contract, their activities in the overseas country are also subject to the general policy guidance of the director of the AID mission. This guidance may, in some cases, limit the ability of the university personnel to carry out the professional assignments made to them by their parent institution.

In fulfilling its responsibilities under such a contract, the American university thus must be prepared for its overseas personnel to undertake work of a character substantially different from their customary responsibilities and to operate under a dual system of academic and non-academic supervision.

Differences in Expectations

The request for an American university to provide technical assistance in the economic aid program ordinarily originates in the overseas AID mission. The reasons which impel the mission director to propose such a technical assistance contract will differ from country to country. However, they usually involve the expectation that the institutional arrangement will enable the mission to provide technical advice in a significant sector of the foreign country's development effort more effectively than by directly engaging individual experts.

AID's desire to reduce its directly employed overseas staff and to implement technical assistance projects through the employment of American consulting firms, professional associations, educational institutions, and other organizations has also stimulated use of university contracts. Many mission directors consider that a university contract offers an opportunity to secure the services of technical assistance experts better qualified than those who can be acquired through direct employment. They also believe that the institution's resources on the home campus will provide a higher level and greater depth of professional support than can be supplied through the technical staffs in AID's Washington headquarters.

In some countries, utilization of a United States university as an instrument of the aid program has been regarded by the mission director (and by the American ambassador) as a new channel for influencing key groups in the foreign community who are inclined to avoid relationships with official American government representatives. They have hoped that American faculty members could help interpret United States foreign policy to intellectual elements of the local scene and could discourage anti-American attitudes and activities among faculty and students of local universities. A few mission directors have also harbored the illusion that provision of technical assistance by an American university, rather than by U.S. government employees, will keep the program out of politics.

At the same time, mission directors are aware that a university contract may complicate their own problems. They appreciate that an American educational institution enters into a contractual arrangement for different reasons than does a profit-making consultant firm. The university's motivation is not only a wish to participate in an important national service activity but also a desire to augment its own institutional competence through the overseas experience. Some American schools have also found AID contracts a useful way of financing the recruitment, training, and utilization of new faculty members pending prospective increases in faculty requirements on the home campus. The primary loyalty of American university personnel, especially when the contract involves institution-to-institution relationships, will be to their home school, rather than to the AID mission. Moreover, they may be inclined to raise questions of institutional prerogatives and academic freedom on matters which would be less significant to other contractors, such as the United States embassy's efforts to involve them in propaganda activities.

Directly employed AID technical advisers deal primarily with the government ministry in their field of work, leaving to the personnel of that ministry the relationship with provincial and local authorities and individual institutions. American professors involved in the improvement of an overseas university under an AID contract usually work with the rector and the faculty of the host university, rather than with the ministry. They sometimes become over-identified with their professional counterparts and come to be active advocates of their clientele's viewpoint, rather than functioning as technical advisors. When differences arise between the local university and the government, the aid mission may be confronted with a situation in which the American university contract group is aggressively supporting the position of the local institution in opposition to the responsible ministry.

The AID mission and the university group often have divergent concepts concerning the role of the university staff. The mission considers that an essential element of the university group's responsibility is that of keeping it, and through it AID's Washington headquarters, regularly informed about the progress of the work under the contract. The programming and legislative cycle of AID is almost a continuous, year-round operation which not only requires periodic detailed reports on all projects but also frequently involves lengthy revisions of project plans and other documents. American faculty members traditionally are impatient even with the modest administrative tasks imposed upon them in their normal work on the home campus, and few of them have any understanding of the reasons for AID's cumbersome requirements. The reporting load, combined with AID's other "paper-work" demands, is regarded by university staff as an undue diversion of their time from their primary task of working with the counterpart institution.

Another variance in role expectancy appears to be developing as AID reduces directly employed technical staffs in its field missions. Mission directors and program officers have fewer AID experts available to them; increasingly they call upon university contract team members for general professional assistance. Occasional requests of this character on matters unrelated to the contract do not represent a major problem. But members of the American faculty tend to regard it as an imposition when they find themselves called upon to function as across-the-board educational advisors to the AID mission at the expense of their work with the host institution.

AID mission directors are harassed men faced with many responsibilities and many demands. The standard AID contract not only provides that the university group shall receive policy guidance from the director, but it also requires the institution to keep him informed about the progress of the project. Serious misunderstandings have developed in some university operations when the director has found that he could not devote as much of his own time to meetings with the chief of an American faculty group as the university representative desired. This communications problem is compounded in a country in which the aid program involves a number of institutional contracts.

One measure adopted by several mission directors to ameliorate this difficulty is to hold periodic conferences with the chiefs of the university parties as a group. These meetings provide an opportunity for exchange of information and for consideration of policy and procedural questions of common concern to the mission and the university teams. Occasionally, awkward general confrontations have ensued between the assembled institutional representatives and the director, but the technique has supplied a valuable forum for mutual consultation, not only between the university groups and the mission, but also among the university representatives themselves.

From the Hosts' Viewpoint

Most host governments have welcomed the use of American universities as suppliers of technical assistance, especially when the contract involves aid to a national educational institution. They usually have been willing to leave to AID the choice of the specific American university to be involved, but in some instances the government or the host institution has insisted that it would only approve arrangements with one of the most prestigious American schools. Acceptance of American technical advisors may, in fact, be regarded by a host government or a host institution as the price to be paid for other forms of aid involved in the project, such as expansion of plant, additional laboratory and other equipment, or opportunities for study visits and fellowships in the United States for faculty members and advanced students.

In many instances the local school considers the teaching of courses for which it lacks adequate faculty as the principal function of the American personnel and is less interested in their ideas about changes in the curriculum, organization, or methods of institutional operation. American faculty members sometimes rep-

resent a threat to the faculty of the host institution. The acceptance of foreign professors may be regarded as evidence of a
failure of the host institution to maintain its own integrity. No
matter how diplomatically the Americans go about their activities,
the local faculty recognize that their underlying purpose is one of
change. Educational institutions everywhere contain groups
opposed to innovation, but when the menace to the traditional
order comes from alien sojourners, cultural differences and
nationalistic attitudes may increase the resistance. On the other
hand, when the key government officials and educational leaders
are convinced of the need for major changes in their country's
system of higher education, they may welcome the innovative
advice and support of United States experts in this field, especially
when these advisers represent an American university, rather than
an official United States government agency.

In a number of instances a foreign school is receiving technical
assistance from several American universities. To some extent
this type of situation is the result of the traditional organization
of AID and its predecessor agencies to program aid to higher education in separate technical fields, such as agriculture, engineering,
health, public administration, and teacher training, without consideration of the general development of the host country's
institutions. But in some cases it also often reflects the attitudes
of overseas universities and their faculties. No American university is equally strong in all the professional and disciplinary areas
in which technical assistance may be required. A foreign school
may not wish to enter into an across-the-board relationship with
one American institution, but prefer to work with the strongest
departments of several different United States universities. Furthermore, few universities abroad have as much or as strong
central direction as do their American counterparts. Their traditional organization is based on individual faculties, each jealous
of its own autonomy and often reluctant to enter into any arrangement, such as a comprehensive contract with a single American
institution, which might tend to strengthen the role of the rector
or other central officer.

People Are Problems

Even when the formal organizational arrangements are satisfactory, conflicts between individuals may impair the success of the enterprise. In an overseas post, difficult people tend to become more difficult. An academic prima donna who is tolerable when he is teaching or doing research in the shelter of his home campus may become impossible when exposed to the strains of an advisory role and to the stresses of living and working in a strange setting. And, as is true for individuals in other occupations, members of a university team who appear well adjusted in their customary surroundings may manifest quite unacceptable behavior when they are stationed in a foreign milieu which lacks some of the social controls of their home environment.

From time to time, interpersonal frictions arise out of relatively petty differences in privileges and status between directly employed mission staff and university contract personnel. The irritations which occur from these causes cut both ways. Mission staff customarily have certain perquisites which usually are not available to contract personnel, such as official passports, use of official commissaries and military mail, U.S. government housing (with air conditioning in tropical climates), and the official social life associated with membership in the local diplomatic community. On the other hand, university contract personnel, in addition to their overseas income-tax exemption, enjoy the prestige and intellectual relationships which other cultures accord to academic personnel, observe university rather than bureaucratic work schedules, and have other advantages attributable to their non-official status. Problems arising from these circumstances usually seem to occur among individuals, in the AID mission or the university group, who are personally poorly suited for overseas work.

Professional snobbism on the part of members of university contract teams may also be a source of difficulty. The education personnel of most AID missions have been selected on the basis of their competence in the development of primary, secondary, and technical education, rather than higher education.

American professors usually do not consider these "public school administrators" qualified to deal with university matters. This attitude naturally is resented by the mission staff, who may regard the university group as arrogant newcomers with little knowledge of the real problems of the country in which they are to work.

How Long Does the University Stay?

Perhaps more fundamental than any of these problems is the inherent difficulty which the mission director faces in appraising the accomplishments under a university contract, and in making recommendations to AID headquarters concerning the renewal of the contract after its initial period. As the Gardner report indicates, some AID officials believe that "no U.S. university ever willingly terminates a contract program, no matter how valid the reasons for doing so."

The mission is under pressure from Washington to secure the establishment of objectives, time-phased targets, and demonstrable results in all activities financed from AID funds. But the real task of an American university in working with a foreign one usually centers upon changes in attitudes and methods of operation which are not readily measured. Modifying traditional patterns of academic thought, organization, and action is a difficult and delicate travail, requiring time and patience. Qualitative achievements in these areas seldom can be scheduled in advance and the most skillful effort may bear tangible fruit only after a long period.

If sound relationships have been established between the American faculty and their colleagues in the host institution, both academic groups ordinarily prefer to see the contract continued. For the host institution, the Americans represent a source of additional instructional staff and an influence for the expansion and improvement of their institution. Those Americans who have made a good personal and professional adjustment to their overseas tasks usually have come to like their work, take pride in the progress they have been able to catalyze, and hope that it can be continued. The American institution usually can point to important problems of the foreign school which require an extension of the contract. The backstopping organization on the home campus sometimes sees such a continuation as the principal justification for its own existence, as well as a matter of university prestige. Assuming that no major reduction in the general level of the assistance program is contemplated by AID, the host government ordinarily has a decisive voice concerning continuation of the contract or the use of the American funds for alternative types of aid.

Some disagreements between the aid mission and the university team concerning continuation of contracts do arise however from differences in perspective. The aid mission basically is concerned with the broad development needs of the host country. The problem it faces is that of how best to utilize the limited sum available for American economic and technical aid so as to obtain the maximum progress toward the development objectives mutually agreed upon between the host country and the United States. The mission director and his staff must decide among the competing claims of various fields of activity. Within an individual field they must select the high priority programs and projects in which American aid can be most effectively employed. They must keep before them the total picture of national development and try to work out with the national authorities the optimal use of available American and local resources.

The American university group, while at least partially aware of the broad development canvas, is primarily concerned with a single local educational institution—or even with only one of its segments. Like other specialists, its members sometimes regard their own focus of interest as the most significant activity in the whole aid program.

The classical macro-micro difference of viewpoint becomes especially acute when, after an initial period of operations, the value of further American financing of assistance to a specific institution is questioned by the mission. The determination of the point at which sufficient external assistance has been provided to assure that the process will continue without further American governmental financing can only be a matter of informed judgment. But that judgment must also be as objective as possible, and it frequently is difficult to obtain such an appraisal from those who have been intimately involved in the contract operation.

Inspection trips by senior representatives of the American institution will provide the mission with some evaluation of performance under the contract, but it is not one which can be regarded as entirely impartial. Study teams of senior representatives from other American schools, or from organizations of schools (perhaps from the accrediting bodies), may provide a solution, but such an arrangement involves delicate and difficult relationships within the American university community.

Research at Your Own Risk?

The traditional intellectual prerogatives of university personnel sometimes give rise to issues between the university group and the mission. The standard AID university contract prohibits any publication by university contract personnel which "would violate the security regulations or be in conflict with the national security of the United States and/or the cooperating government." Furthermore any proposed publication must be submitted to AID thirty days in advance. Academics tend to develop and maintain their professional prestige through their writings and usually have an occupational compulsion to share widely the knowledge they have acquired in their research and their experience. While most university personnel would recognize the need to protect United States national security, they are not inclined to accept some subordinate official's judgment as to whether a proposed publication actually does involve the national security.

Many of the disputes which have arisen in relation to publication have involved potential embarrassment to American foreign relations, rather than national security as such. An American professor who has observed corruption, injustice, or governmental stupidity in the country in which he has been working under an AID-financed contract often considers that he has a duty to write about it upon his return home. He may appreciate that when his critical book or magazine article reaches the country, the American ambassador, the AID mission director, and his own university colleagues who have remained behind, can expect heated protests from the national authorities and a period of some acerbity in relationships. But the individualistic faculty member may not consider that he has any responsibility for intergovernmental comity or even for the continuation of a cooperative climate for his university's overseas project. He may regard these objectives as of lesser importance than increasing and diffusing knowledge about overseas phenomena.

The publication issue usually involves the writings of members of the American university team after they have left the country, rather than during their stay. However, the desire of faculty members to undertake research into local situations beyond that authorized in the contract can be another source of friction, both with the aid mission and with the host government. Action-minded administrators of economic assistance assume that the task of university faculty is to get on with the institutional development and teaching work which has already been agreed upon in the contract, rather than devote their time to new research. The director of the aid mission frequently feels that more information is already available about the country's problems than he can possibly use.

If the mission considers that a proposed research activity is irrelevant to the contract, the university staff may question the professional competence of the AID staff member to pass upon the pertinence of their search for knowledge, or even challenge the mission's right to raise the question so long as the research does not interfere with the performance of the work specified in the contract. National (and academic) authorities in developing countries often are unaccustomed to many of the types of social science research which interest American professors. They may become suspicious of the motivations for certain kinds of studies and surmise that they are part of a United States intelligence operation. Moreover, every nation has its neglected problems and failures which government leaders may prefer to leave undisturbed, at least for the moment.

Meanwhile, Back on the Campus

The nature of the American university's home campus organization for supporting and serving its overseas personnel often depends upon whether the institution's contracts involve only one, or several, disciplinary or professional fields. AID's most recent list of university contracts indicates that in most cases the agency has continued its predecessors' practice of contracting for American schools to collaborate with overseas institutions in a single specified area, such as agriculture, engineering, teacher training, or public administration. Fewer than a dozen of the 143 contracts in operation on June 30, 1965, appear to cover several fields or to be concerned with the general institutional development of the foreign university.

An American institution which enters into several AID contracts involving technical assistance in different fields to various overseas schools will probably see little need for a central unit in its own organization to support and service the field teams provided under these contracts. Instead, it usually will designate a "campus coordinator" for each contract, locating the possessor of this horrendous title in the department or school most directly concerned with the substantive aspects of the contractual program. The standard AID contract specifies that he is to be the institution's representative "for coordinating the overseas and home campus activities carried out under the contract."

The campus coordinator seldom is a senior member of the faculty. Much of his time is devoted to the administrative and financial details of contract operation and to field mission logistics, rather than to substantive matters. If he is to secure the participation of the most experienced members of his department or school faculty in providing program advice to the field group or in recruiting personnel for overseas service, he must have strong support from the dean or department head.

Some American universities have established a central institution-wide backstopping service for overseas contract operations. This has proved an especially valuable step for institutions whose contracts involve technical assistance in several fields to the same overseas university. An organizational unit of this character serves as the general representative of the university in its contractual relationships with AID. It develops special skill in the negotiation and administration of contracts and in working with the business side of the university on financial, procurement, and other problems. It also functions as a coordinating service for the various elements concerned in the university's contractual commitment, especially on problems involving the general development of the overseas institution. Such an office generally is headed by a high ranking member of the university's academic staff, who has the prestige necessary to secure the active cooperation of senior faculty members and administrative officers throughout the institution. He usually is also wise enough to place major stress upon maintaining the responsibility of the individual professional schools and disciplinary departments for the planning of the substantive aspects of technical assistance in their respective fields and for the provision of qualified members for the university's overseas teams.

A central unit of this nature may be useful in the American university, even if all its contractual relationships with overseas institutions are in different substantive areas. Departments and schools in most American institutions of higher education tend to be conservative rather than innovative. Their primary interests usually center about the education of American students and the personal research activities of individual faculty members. They need to be stimulated by vigorous leadership to devote attention to the relationships with an overseas institution. Sometimes this leadership exists within the department or school, but in many universities the development of forward-looking ideas about the adaptation of American experience in foreign environments, the formulation of imaginative new research programs, and the evolution of methods for bringing the fruits of overseas work to the home campus requires a catalytic agent outside the departmental organization.

The central backstopping organization may expand into a general international programs unit concerned with a broad spectrum of the university's international activities in addition to AID-financed contracts. It can develop a special expertise in identifying significant gaps in the institution's world affairs and cross-cultural activities. It can help to bring about the collaboration of diverse departments and schools in teaching, research, and service activities focused upon major problems of common concern, such as the economic and social development of low-income countries. It can aid in the establishment of meaningful interdisciplinary area study programs related to the institution's overseas commitments and take leadership in the development of inter-university consortia and other techniques by which several institutions with similar or complementary interests can operate in an integrated fashion. And it can also direct attention to important problems which may otherwise fall between the interstices in university structure, such as the role of indigenous universities in the political, economic, and cultural development of new countries or the problem of training foreign graduate students to become effective instructors when they return to their home institutions.

Many of these activities need not be undertaken directly by the central unit itself. Its major purpose should be to help build awareness of the university's international responsibilities into all the schools and departments. It usually can function more effectively if it serves as a communications nexus and a center of stimulation and coordination for other parts of the university and assists in securing the resources necessary to enable the schools and departments to enlarge their international dimensions. To function in this fashion, such a unit requires the active support of the principal officers of the university.

One of the important concerns of a central international unit can be the development of improved methods of preparing members of the university's faculty for overseas assignments. As educational institutions, American universities have often been critical of the official orientation courses provided for federal government personnel who are to be stationed abroad. But with the recent improvements in the training programs of some of the military services, the State Department, and AID, these government agencies may be doing more competent and innovative work in this area than are many universities.

Most large American institutions have on their own campuses a variety of expertise in such fields as cross-cultural operations, comparative higher education and educational administration, and personal and family adjustment to new environments. In many cases they also possess comprehensive area knowledge about the countries in which they have institutional interests and facilities for instruction in the languages of such countries. But only a few of the institutions which have undertaken AID contracts are adequately utilizing their own resources to make sure that their representatives are equipped to function effectively in overseas relationships or even to understand the differences in philosophy, organization, and methods of operation between institutions of higher education in the United States and those of other countries. Some universities do not "debrief" returning members of the their field groups in any organized fashion. The information and experience of these veterans not only is grist for the preparation of their successors but represents a most valuable source of ideas for program development, both overseas and on the home campus. A central international programs unit obviously can serve these institution-wide needs more effectively than can a series of individual coordinators in several schools and departments.

Evaluation in depth of university contract operations is dealt with in the paper by Edward Weidner elsewhere in this collection. In addition to formal terminal appraisal, the administration of an overseas program also involves periodic supervisory and inspectional visits by personnel from the home campus. One of the compensations of the harassed campus coordinator is that of periodic trips to the field to review with the overseas group the status of their work and to assist in any problems involving the American embassy or the AID mission. These trips afford the field group opportunity to discuss progress and difficulties with a headquarters representative on a face-to-face basis. They also furnish the home campus with the information it needs to understand probable developments in the contractual relationships, future personnel needs, and other requirements. The co-ordinator also gains comprehension of the real significance of the formalistic language used in official AID documents, which should serve him well in the negotiation of contract amendments and extensions in Washington.

The development of institution-to-institution relationships is facilitated through field trips by high ranking American university representatives. The head of a foreign university will ordinarily expect to be visited by the head of the American institution, or at least by the dean or department chairman most directly concerned with the subject-matter field involved in the contract. Through these protocol visits the American field group may be able to make progress on sticky issues with the head of the host institution or with high levels of the host government. Visiting university presidents and deans often are also able to reinforce the relationships of their overseas staffs with the American ambassador or the AID mission director, if this is necessary. The appearance of such academic dignitaries is evidence, both to the members of the university's own overseas group and to the host institution, of the American school's high level interest in the progress of the collaborative task. Unfortunately these travelers seldom are able to stay in the country long enough to make a substantial contribution to local thinking about the fundamental problems of governmental and institutional planning and organization for higher education.

Time Now for a Fresh Approach

Other parts of this symposium deal with the need for substantial changes in the present arrangement under which most university work overseas is financed. AID contracts are relatively short term and are subject to the shifting fortunes of the foreign aid program which may be inconsistent with the university relationship. Some longer range system obviously is required. AID has now had sufficient experience to appreciate the time-span required to secure fundamental changes in developing countries, especially when the innovations disturb traditional systems. As the source of financing, it also has a right to assure itself that its agent, the American university, has a well-considered strategy for accomplishing the agreed upon objectives of the contract, and that the effort put forth at home and abroad is directed toward the achievement of these objectives.

Such a new system might be based upon the separate institute for educational and technical cooperation suggested by the Gardner report or upon one of the several alternatives which have been discussed. In any event, it should provide the framework within which American universities and host institutions may build broad and continuing interrelationships. Under a system of this character the American schools would be able to make orderly plans for incorporating overseas assignments in their faculty development programs, and to develop orientation and training facilities for prospective field staff members on a sound educational basis. The quality of American university representation thus would improve greatly.

The longer term basis for university work would tend to alleviate many of the substantive and administrative problems involved in present overseas contract operations. Relationships with the host institutions would not be focused upon the subject matter areas of interest to the U.S. foreign assistance program, but might encompass all the fields in which the two institutions have a mutuality of interest. The partnership and feedback aspects of the relationship could be developed more intensively, since one of the recognized elements in such a program would be the enhancement of the capabilities of the American university. The American institution could also organize its home campus activities on a solid basis to assure that the intellectual resources available in its various departments and schools are utilized whenever they can contribute to the enterprise.

The nature of the relationships between the American university's field representatives and official American agencies in the overseas country would be quite different from the present pattern. So long as public funds of the United States are the primary source of financial support for the American institution's overseas work, the governmental authorities have a right to assurance that they are expended for the purpose for which they were supplied. Moreover, the American ambassador would still have responsibility for seeing that the university's operations were not working to the detriment of major U.S. foreign policy objectives. But the university's activities would be less immediately identified with other aid-financed programs designed to yield short-term results. The American faculty would not attempt to maintain its present Janus-like posture between the host institution and the AID mission, but instead would concentrate its attention upon working with its collaborators in the overseas school.

Most important of all, under a long-range system, the American university would be in the position of organizing its overseas activities as an integral part of its own institutional development program. This would permit it to select those programs and projects which are most significant to the university's rounded growth, rather than to manage a series of opportunistic undertakings chosen almost without an institutional frame of reference.

James A. McCain
Arthur D. Weber

The Faculty Expatriate

International activities have added a major new dimension to American higher education. What with their involvement in scores of technical assistance programs in developing nations, foreign student enrollments approaching the 100,000 mark, summer institutes and junior-year-abroad centers in a score of foreign countries, and the accelerating flow of scholars across national boundaries for international conferences or appointments as guest lecturers, our campuses will never be the same again.

Of all this variety of global activity, the strongest and, hopefully, the worthiest impact on the university might be expected from the "faculty expatriate" when he returns to his job personally enriched and professionally broadened by firsthand exposure to a foreign culture from a year or more of foreign service. Too little has been done to date to evaluate systematically the experiences of these faculty members abroad or their influence after their homecoming. But it seems safe to assume that, unlike the foreign service officers lampooned in *The Ugly American,* most of them have exploited the opportunity for close association with the people of their host countries, often at the sacrifice of comfort and health.

The objective of this paper is twofold: First, to discuss how and why overseas service affects the faculty member and his university; and secondly, to consider what might be done to improve and strengthen the faculty expatriate's contributions to academic programs and the academic community.

78

"Faculty Expatriate" Defined

At the outset, it seems appropriate to define the term *faculty expatriate* in the context of this discussion. Generally speaking, *expatriate* has unsavory connotations. Webster defines expatriate as "an exile; a person who withdraws from his own country to live in another country." Fiction writers, Oliver LaFarge for example, sometimes epitomize the expatriate as a dissolute individual who has become so involved with native spirits (alcohol) and women that he loses his university ties, falls behind in his research and other work, and eventually, cast off by his home campus, "goes native." [1] Then there is the academic "bum" or professional foreign mercenary. This is the faculty expatriate who for various reasons, personal and professional, has volunteered for numerous overseas assignments under diverse sponsorships. He has lost what limited touch he once had with American higher education; he has hopped from one program to another, either looking for an impossibly romantic and glamorous assignment or hoping to escape from his past failures and frustrations. [2]

Such repugnant types may make exciting copy for popular fiction, but the aberrant is not the expatriate with whom this paper deals. Our primary concern is the faculty member whose professional service overseas is sponsored or approved by his own university. He continues to be associated with his university either directly or on the basis of an approved leave without pay. Presumably, his background, education, training, experiences, and skills were, or should have been, taken into account when he was recruited for the assignment.

Prior to the 1940's the foreign experiences of American college professors were predominantly European and were comprised mainly of sabbatical tours or research projects undertaken

[1] Oliver LaFarge, *The Door in the Wall* (Boston: Houghton Mifflin Company, 1965), pp. 19-39.

[2] Campus Coordinators Conference, Proceedings, 1963, Fort Collins, Colorado, August 1963, p. 12.

abroad.[3] Although the ranks of expatriate professors in technical assistance programs have mushroomed within the last decade, there are always, in addition to these, several hundred professors from American universities involved in other kinds of work overseas under the employ of the United States government or that of the host country. Many of them teach or engage in research under the Fulbright or Smith-Mundt Acts. The Maryland Armed Forces Program, hiring through the University of Maryland, employs professors to teach throughout Europe.[4]

Nongovernment sources also employ American professors for overseas work. The Rockefeller and Ford foundations sponsor a large-scale exchange of professors in the humanities between American and European universities, and the Carnegie and Guggenheim foundations make grants to American professors desiring to do research in foreign countries.[5] Another contribution of faculty members to international development comes through the services of those granted leave to accept special assignments with such international organizations as FAO, WHO, private foundations, and government agencies in foreign lands.[6] American professors are also employed as instructors by European corporations having management training centers, e.g., the IPSOA school in Turin, financed by the Fiat and Olivetti companies, and the IMEDE school at Lausanne, sponsored by the Nestlé Company.[7]

There were 3,793 United States faculty members abroad during the academic year 1964-65 doing research or teaching in 108 countries.[8] There were 3,400 the previous year.[9] More than half

[3] Harlan Cleveland, Gerard J. Mangone, and John Clarke Adams, *The Overseas Americans* (New York: McGraw-Hill Book Company, 1960), p. 194.

[4] Walter Adams and John A. Garraty, *From Main Street to the Left Bank* (East Lansing: Michigan State University Press, 1959), p. 152.

[5] *Ibid.*, p. 154.

[6] Charles E. Palm, "Challenges and Opportunities of a Land-Grant Institution in Foreign Agricultural Work" (Ithaca: Cornell International Agricultural Development Monograph, 1962), p. 6. (Mimeographed.)

[7] Adams and Garraty, *From Main Street to the Left Bank*, p. 154.

[8] *Bulletin on International Education,* July-August 1965, p. 4.

[9] Institute of International Education, *Open Doors, 1963-64* (New York: The Institute, 1964), p. 4.

of these expatriates were involved in research and teaching in the humanities and social sciences; [10] approximately five percent of them were engaged in agricultural technical assistance programs.[11] The University of California leads the field in number of professors working overseas, with a total of 225 for the year 1963-64; Michigan State and Columbia follow closely behind. Fourteen American universities had forty or more expatriate staff members in 1963-64.[12]

Potential Problem Expatriates

Not all faculty expatriates are recruited; some are eager volunteers. Among them are a few who are unhappy or dissatisfied with their personal situations on the home campus. They are looking for relief; the farther they can get from their problems and frustrations, the better satisfied they think they will be. Some may have justifiable reasons for complaint, but a foreign assignment is unlikely to remove the causes of their dissatisfaction. When they return and resume their regular university duties they often find adjustment difficult. They are restless and uneasy in a situation which they feel has worsened, not improved as they had hoped, during their absence. Having become expatriates for the wrong reasons, they return extolling the advantages of the foreign country where they served and complaining because they are not appreciated and rewarded at home.

Some professors see only their own edification and enrichment as a goal in overseas service and decry the need for institutionalization of the procedures involved. "Must we rob all experience of spontaneity and the excitement of adventure?" was the plaint of one expatriate professor in answer to questions concerning his preparation for the assignment and plans for utilizing his experiences. His cry undoubtedly has echoes from many other

[10] *Bulletin on International Education,* July-August 1965, p. 5.

[11] *Open Doors,* p. 15.

[12] *Ibid.,* p. 11.

expatriate professors who nostalgically recall their overseas experiences as charming interludes free from the pressures or boredom of their normal academic routines.

Because of what they are and the way they react to situations at home and abroad, these types contribute to the faculty expatriate problem even though they may have served creditably as expatriates.

Another relatively small group of faculty expatriates might be categorized as *reluctant recruits*. Their universities often are deeply involved in international programs; their administrative superiors admonish them to be ready to accept foreign assignments when their turns come. Their involvement may be a matter of loyalty to the university rather than a personal commitment to the program.

The overseas performance of such expatriates may not reflect their personal reservations about the program, particularly if the official commitment of the university is recognized and respected by the faculty generally. But if this commitment or the motive back of it is in doubt or questioned, the reluctant recruit may feel that he is being exiled.

Gardner identified this concern of the faculty expatriate when he wrote: "The university man overseas wants to feel (and act as though) he has the whole weight and dignity of his institution behind him, but he is often functioning virtually as an independent operator, and his university has committed itself only superficially. Functioning thus independently, he may or may not behave in a way that conforms with the integrity and responsibility of a great university." [13] Certainly, a remark, facetious or otherwise, by a university president or a dean about solving a personnel problem by sending a staff member overseas would appear to support this contention and tend to destroy confidence in the university's commitment to an international program.

[13] John W. Gardner, *AID and the Universities,* Report from Education and World Affairs in Cooperation with the Agency for International Development (New York: Education and World Affairs, 1964), p. 37.

The University and Its Expatriates

The attitudes and the policies of university administrators do have an important bearing on the ultimate role of the faculty expatriate. The faculty expatriate's performance during and after his absence from the campus often is an indication of overall university commitment and dedication to this new international dimension of higher education. The conditions of his recruitment, home campus support of the program for which he is responsible, and the recognition given for his service and accomplishments are the real measures of the university commitment.

When the entire university administration and faculty are genuinely interested in and concerned about world affairs and international education programs, they will applaud the efforts and the accomplishments of their colleagues who serve overseas. In such an environment *expatriate* is rarely used to designate the faculty member who serves in a foreign country, for the connotation associated with his service is laudable and pleasant, not unsavory.

There is an increasing number of universities throughout the United States where this enlightened viewpoint toward world affairs and international education prevails. And most, perhaps all, university administrators would disclaim any intent, official or otherwise, to achieve any other objective. Yet, a realistic appraisal indicates that much remains to be done to enable the faculty expatriate to make the most significant contribution to the academic community.

That there are problems and inadequacies in regard to university staffing of overseas projects is certainly no indictment of the hundreds of dedicated professors who have made contributions to education and development in all parts of the world. Nor is it even surprising if the traditional role of the American university and its brief history of participation in overseas programs are considered. However, considering the large number of American professors involved in overseas programs and recognizing the fact that university commitment to overseas service is a growing concern,[14] it seems appropriate, if not imperative, that the American university expend serious effort to construct an overall rationale to improve the overseas performance of the expatriate professor and to insure the return of his resultant knowledge and experiences to proper avenues of beneficial application within his own university. Gardner emphasized in his report that: "The universities have not done anything like an adequate job of producing men with solid professional preparation for work in some aspect of development, and they must apply themselves to this task." [15]

The Screening Process

If the academic American is to make his best contribution to better international understanding and development, he must be selected, regardless of shortages, with far more discrimination in the future than in the past.

Certain obvious liabilities may be eliminated at the outset by clarifying the "Ugly American" [16] and "Silent American" [17] characteristics which infuriate and baffle the countrymen of foreign lands. And those professors who feel constrained to "bear the white man's burden," those who "go native," and those who flash their "wealth" to impress the natives [18] are poor representatives of the ideals and aims of the American university. These individuals typify a hazard of foreign service which should not be ignored by those responsible for the role of the university in world affairs. Granted that early identification of such individuals is difficult, benefits to the total United States overseas program amply justify special care be taken to assure screening out during

[14] For example, Sir Alexander M. Carr-Saunders in his report to the Tananarive Conference calculated that more than 5,000 expatriate teachers would be needed in the Middle African universities alone in the twenty-year period from 1960 to 1980. "Staffing African Universities," (London: Overseas Development Institute, 1963), p. 10.

[15] Gardner, *AID and the Universities,* p. 37.

[16] William J. Lederer and Eugene Burdick, *The Ugly American* (New York: Norton, 1956).

[17] Donald Lloyd, "The Quietmouth American," *Harper's,* September 1963, pp. 101-105.

[18] Walter Adams and John A. Garraty, *Is the World Our Campus?* (East Lansing: Michigan State University Press, 1960), p. 79.

selection all those who are likely to discredit themselves and the institutions they represent.

It would be a serious oversight to neglect the importance of the wife and family of the expatriate professor. The ability of his wife to set up and maintain a comfortable refuge in the midst of every conceivable household annoyance and upheaval occasioned by unfamiliar and adverse circumstances can and has made the difference between a successful career for a professor or a quiet but final dismissal as an incompetent technician. Some overseas wives complain about the "irregular water supply, the erratic electricity," the daily battle with uncomprehending servants and against hepatitis, mononucleosis, and dysentery.[19] Some find the life so lacking in stimulating pursuits that they continually threaten to pack up and go home; some do. The expatriate professor whose wife accepts the facts of life as she finds them and proceeds to make the best home possible in spite of complications, has the best chance not only for success in his work, but for finding unexpected pleasure and rewards from his foreign sojourn.

The criticism has been made by certain expatriate professors that they were humiliated by the attitudes and actions of their fellow expatriates. The academic American has on occasion conveyed a distorted image of American higher education to a foreign audience already prejudiced by American movies, bold-face scandal headlines, and irresponsible tourists. Thus, the American university is sometimes reproached by foreign university officials. Typical was the complaint of one such official: "We had faith in Americans—their kindness, humility, and generosity. But our hopes were soon crushed when we realized that the professors sent to us were not the first rate scholars that had been promised, but mediocrities, who seemed more concerned with getting diplomatic license plates for their cars, buying Scotch at bargain-counter commissary prices, and joining the social whirl of the cocktail circuit, than with helping our country to develop."[20]

There are few reliable figures available to indicate how many expatriate professors have succeeded and how many have failed.

[19] *Ibid.,* p. 70.   [20] *Ibid.,* pp. 66, 67.

In some instances, rather than risk adverse publicity, a university administration has waited until the end of a period of service before quietly terminating its obligations to an incompetent or morally unfit expatriate. Some expatriates have indeed earned bitter condemnation. It should be obvious that unsuitable personnel in foreign assignments jeopardize not only American prestige, but also the reputation of the sponsoring university. The financial investment alone would be a serious economic disadvantage to a university whose expatriate staff members must be fired or shipped home.

Screening the misfits out of overseas service is important, but this unpleasant necessity can be avoided by painstaking recruitment practices.[21] The greatest drawback in selection is the simple fact that selection and training are regarded as two different actions.[22] The university or government recruiting agency has consistently first hired and then briefed for the specific assignment. On the other hand, if training were regarded as a part of the recruitment process, a screening out of the weakest prospects would be facilitated. Those who survive a brief training period in which attitudes are tested while skills are learned would in all probability possess the values and character attributes necessary for working overseas.[23]

If the faculty expatriate is a problem to the university, the problem has come about in part at least because the university itself has not had a well-conceived program dealing with international education and world affairs. In back of the unsavory connotations associated with the term *faculty expatriate* are the university's own practices and policies. When these are improved, those on foreign duty will not be thought of as expatriates. Ideally, most, perhaps all, faculty members will have had overseas experience. When this happens, the conditions of overseas service, not the fact of it, will get major emphasis and attention at American universities.

[21] Cleveland *et al., The Overseas Americans,* p. 169.
[22] *Ibid.,* p. 187.
[23] *Ibid.*

The Conditions of Assignment

The exigencies of working in a new and strange environment with transcultural complexities of communication and values have been extensively described in a wealth of literature on technical assistance projects. Suffice it to say here that sometimes the attractive salaries and other perquisites offered for such employment are not enough to induce an American professor who is successful on the home campus to pull up stakes and go abroad for even a two-year period. Frequently the criticism is heard from American professors that going on overseas assignments results in their being slighted when raises in salary and promotions are being considered and that other opportunities are lost, such as chances for better jobs, speaking opportunities, consulting assignments, and so on. In overseas positions they lack the laboratory equipment and library resources to carry on new and interesting research in their fields, thus retarding their own educational progress and putting them behind their colleagues when they return to their home campuses.

Before the faculty member goes overseas, the conditions of his appointment and its effect on his faculty status should be set forth in specific detail and agreed upon. If his duties are to be different when he returns, the changes should be discussed and agreed upon before, not after, he has accepted the overseas assignment. There have been instances where the university staff member would not have accepted such an appointment had he known when he did so that his status would be changed when he returned. In any case, confidence in the university's commitment to foreign programs is impaired when such situations arise.

Another reason for dissatisfaction and frustration among faculty abroad stems from failure to be rewarded for meritorious overseas service by salary increases and advances in rank. Though a salary differential usually is paid during the foreign assignment, this does not take the place of annual increases in the base salary paid for regular service on the home campus. When the base salary remains the same for the duration of the foreign tour of duty and advances in rank are withheld or postponed, the staff member questions whether overseas service is, in fact, rated equally with domestic teaching, research, and extension. And if he is told that further increases and advances must wait until he brings himself up-to-date in his specialty through additional experience on the home campus, he is unlikely to be an advocate of foreign service when he resumes his regular duties. If there is a good reason for leaving the base salary and faculty rank unchanged, as might possibly be true in the case of a young inexperienced staff member, this should be understood and agreed upon in advance.

Another practice which is sometimes misunderstood both at home and abroad, and thus may affect international programs adversely, relates to temporary advances in rank for faculty expatriates. For example, an assistant professor may be given the temporary rank of full professor while serving overseas. This might be a concession to a rank conscious host country when the American university finds it difficult to recruit or to release full professors for foreign service. This practice also has been justified in terms of the host country's stage of development and its need for basic, as opposed to advanced, technical assistance.[24] The risk, of course, is that as the practice becomes known and publicized in the host country and on the home campus, confidence in the program will be weakened and more will be lost than gained.

Academic rank is not the only source of problems associated with the use of younger staff members in international programs. In some fields, especially the physical and biological sciences, advances are being made so rapidly that there is a real question whether a young man can afford to interrupt his research and devote two years or longer to a foreign assignment where it is

[24] Some foreign countries reveal the sensitivity of their newly developing status by insisting on unrealistic standards in the academic rank and prestige of the personnel acceptable to them. It thus becomes difficult if not impossible to fill their demands from the available American professors and technicians prepared for a foreign assignment. On the other hand, some foreign officials balk at the high degree of preparation of American professors. President Nyerere of Tanganyika was troubled by the big gap between preferred technical help and his country's ability to use it. "High powered expert advisers," he explained, are often an embarrassment, because his countrymen cannot apply or absorb highly sophisticated skills. As quoted in Luis Munoz Marin, "The Human Element in Foreign Assistance," *Sixth World Conference Proceedings, Society for International Development* (Washington: The Society, March 1964), p. 19.

unlikely that he will be able to keep abreast of developments in his specialty. During his absence he will be working under a different situation entirely and confronted with totally different problems from those that he has faced at home. Laboratory facilities will be inadequate or lacking entirely, and he may be so busy that he will have little time to think about his teaching assignments and the research projects on the home campus. This would be serious enough, but even more disconcerting to the young staff member is the fact that he may not be able to publish or keep up with new findings published by others in his field.

In addition to such drawbacks of a one- or two-year foreign assignment for younger staff members, universities are being urged to make their senior staff members available for as much as five years' duty as project leaders.[25] The contention is that this is required if a really significant contribution is to be made. One must become acquainted with the culture of a country and its problems before he can be fully effective. Furthermore, it takes time and patience to win the confidence of persons in positions of authority in the host country who can bring about needed changes. Yet, such a five-year absence might seriously impair the staff member's qualifications for effective service on the home campus. But should he be penalized when he returns? Or should special provision be made for his reentry to normal faculty duties? It may well be that with more experience in international programs, American universities will remedy this situation by making it possible for the staff member to continue his research while away from the campus. More frequent visits to the home campus might be provided for.

It would be most unfortunate if staff members eventually should be penalized for their dedicated service overseas. It has been pointed out that going overseas on a technical assistance mission "has often posed a choice between a trip of such short duration as to be of questionable value to the host country and

[25] F. F. Hill, "Organizing to Help Establish and Strengthen Agricultural Institutions in Developing Countries." Paper read before Section (O) Agriculture of the American Association for the Advancement of Science, Cleveland, Ohio, December 30, 1963 (New York: Ford Foundation). (Mimeographed.)

one long enough to impose real personal penalties." [26] And Gardner has stressed that the way to avoid this difficulty is to root out the "attitude that overseas activities are something quite separate from the mainstream of the university's life and being." [27]

Expatriates Speak of the Problems

In considering what might be done to improve and strengthen the faculty expatriate's contributions to academic programs and the academic community, the authors wrote 1,144 faculty members who were listed by 36 universities in 22 states as having had foreign experience. Of 438 replies received at the time this paper was being written, 159 were not tabulated for the following reasons: (1) Only foreign experience was army service; (2) born in foreign country, but professional experience in the United States only; (3) served less than one year overseas; and (4) overseas experience not university-related.

Effectiveness of Orientation Programs

We asked these faculty expatriates: "Were you given any special orientation prior to your overseas assignment? If so, what, where, and by whom?" Of the 279 replies summarized, only 148, or 53 percent of the respondents, reported that they had received orientation before going overseas. The orientation sessions that were reported upon ranged from one day to about two weeks and for the most part were held on the home campuses and in Washington. In a few instances, special orientation was given in the countries to which the faculty members were assigned.

Comments were almost unanimous that the orientation on administrative procedures and personal matters concerned with travel, health, etc., was much more adequate than that relating to the duties and responsibilities of the faculty member in the

[26] Dael Wolfle, "Foreign Programs for Universities," Editorial, *Science*, July 17, 1964.

[27] Gardner, *AID and the Universities*, p. 10.

country to which he was assigned. This was emphasized by such statements as:

"Orientation on technical matters was of little value."

"I had to learn my job after I got there."

"Advance information on my role as an advisor was sketchy and inadequate."

"Orientation was inadequate for my special assignment."

"At ———— University interest in and information for orientation are lacking."

"Entirely too much 'hogwash' has been given to orientation needs."

These comments agree with the results of a study by Guthrie and Spencer.[28] They reported that "there was virtually no orientation to the details of the assignment. Some consultants were able to find persons who had served abroad in the same profession and in the same country and to gain from them some details of what the work actually involved. There was usually a rather sketchy statement of the task in the possession of the recruiter. Very often he had not been in the country concerned, and equally frequently he was not a member of the same profession as the man approached."

Many respondents indicated disappointment in the orientation received in Washington. Typical comments were:

"Of limited value."

"Poor."

"Disappointing."

"A waste of time."

"Too general."

"No good; they had not been there."

"Three-day briefing by arm-chair experts was of no value."

"Orientation had little to do with the program."

"Not very helpful."

"Four days in Washington, D. C., were utterly wasted."

---

[28] George M. Guthrie and Richard E. Spencer, "American Professors and Overseas Technical Assistance" (University Park: Pennsylvania State University, 1965), p. 31.

The Delhi Training and Orientation Centre for Foreign Technicians in India was commented upon very favorably by those who had participated in its seminars. This Centre was established within the Delhi School of Economics, University of Delhi, with the joint financial support of the Ford Foundation and the United States Technical Cooperation Mission (now the Agency for International Development). The purpose of the Delhi Training and Orientation Centre, as set forth in a brochure distributed with the program of its forty-fourth seminar, is to instruct recently arrived foreign technicians on Indian culture and economic and social development. The rationale for the Centre's program was explained in these words:

> Foreign technicians and members of the foreign technical and other missions coming to India have for a long time requested and required an organized, guided, and intensive study of India, its history, culture, its customs, and programmes for development, as a necessary preparation for the work they have come to do. While technicians sent to India have been given some preparatory orientation on India, it has been recognized that the studies could be conducted with far more effectiveness in India itself. For, here in India, they could see for themselves the people and the country they are studying; here they could make field trips, and have the benefit of personal instruction from India's leaders and specialists.
>
> The Centre organizes six two-week seminar courses a year. In addition to these courses the Centre also has planned some special courses. These seminars include lectures on India's cultural heritage, religions, languages, arts, economics, health, education, planning, and social life and customs. One full day is given to village life in India and includes a visit to a village. Class discussions, with ample opportunity for participation of the group, and field trips are scheduled as important parts of the course. . . . Movies are also shown to make the subject matter more vivid. . . . All persons who have attended the courses at the Orientation Centre may use the library (about 25,000 volumes on India), and between the intensive courses, they may take books from the library for a short period.[29]

In addition to the seminar program of the Delhi Training and Orientation Centre, special orientation is provided for American

---

[29] "The Delhi Training and Orientation Centre for Foreign Technicians in India" (Delhi: University of Delhi, 1960).

personnel by the United States Mission in New Delhi. In these sessions emphasis is placed on the role of foreign technicians and the function and operation of the embassy and its technical assistance and other programs in India.

Though resources available in India for an orientation program are unique and perhaps could be duplicated in few developing countries where United States technical assistance is being given, the seminars of the Delhi Training and Orientation Centre provide some useful guidelines for orientation programs irrespective of where they are held or how they are sponsored. A few respondents to our questionnaire who have not served in India and may not even have heard about orientation seminars there, made recommendations suggesting the objectives and procedures of the Delhi Training and Orientation Centre. The consensus seemed to be that improved orientation programs would result from the greater use of foreign graduate students and faculty members with experience in the country for which orientation is being given.

Some respondents stressed the complexity as well as the importance of orientation for foreign service in statements such as this:

> Orientation, I believe, should consist of more than physical and material suggestions. It should include briefing in a country's politics, educational patterns, development statistics, and national psychology, as well as culture. Language study is also an essential. . . . If Americans—amateurs in the international field as we are—do not learn the art and the practice of overseas service more efficiently than can be done by trial and error, we shall remain amateurs, and we will make too many mistakes.

Quoting again from the Gardner report:

> Today all too many contract personnel go overseas with no previous experience, stay just long enough to begin to learn their jobs, and then return home, never to work abroad again. It is essential that we have a large reservoir of trained and experienced people who have been on such assignments before and have already accomplished much of the necessary learning (e.g. knowledge of the language, familiarity with problems of operating overseas, a 'feel' for the pace and style of

another society). Such people . . . could move with competence and rapidly into particular overseas assignments.[30]

One respondent implied that the orientation job is too big for the individual university when he stated that "there is need for a nationwide orientation program for contract as well as direct-hire AID employees."

Avenues for Feedback

No respondent mentioned that orientation was available for the specific purpose of preparing him to use his overseas experiences after he returned. This is not surprising, perhaps, since feedback to the university from projects abroad has received little attention until recently.

On the other hand, as pointed out in the Gardner report:

> The lessons learned from the [overseas] experience should not go unrecorded. Many of these lessons are only available in the minds of faculty participants, and if no funds are to be had, that's where they may remain. If time and money are available, these people will do what comes naturally for university faculty—convert their insights into new curriculum, research, articles, and books. Such a harvest should be part of any well-conceived project.[31]

The feedback question was discussed at length at a recent seminar sponsored by the American Council on Education. These excerpts from the Summary Proceedings of that seminar are apropos to the subject of this paper:

> Integrated with the discussion of staffing was the question of feedback from projects abroad. How does an institution use the experience gained from overseas activities in its total program? Does it gain less feedback when mercenaries are employed—a principal reason given by those who objected to the practice? Answers to these questions varied widely. Feedback will be varied in any case, but there is bound to be feedback since the individual will bring back his own experiences. It is not altogether a question of the individual using his own experience in his teaching and research, however, for the feedback is not

[30] Gardner, *AID and the Universities,* p. 34.

[31] *Ibid.,* p. 30.

necessarily of value from the university's point of view unless it is applicable to the institution's program.[32]

Dangerfield associated the feedback problem with inadequate preparation for orientation to the foreign assignment when he said:

> Too many of us have contracts in which we send qualified personnel abroad, they serve as qualified personnel, they come back as qualified personnel, but because they were unprepared to gain from the experience, they haven't profited. We can send a brilliant engineer to India; he can serve brilliantly; he can return to the campus as a brilliant engineer, and yet the little he has learned about India is often wrong. He is not conditioned to learn about Indian culture.[33]

Our letter addressed to faculty members with foreign experience requested information on feedback from overseas programs. As the basis for comments and suggestions, we asked: "Since resuming your regular duties at your university after serving abroad, what opportunities have you had to share your knowledge and experiences with colleagues, students, and others? Does your university emphasize 'feedback' from university-related programs and technical assistance projects in other countries? If so, how is this being accomplished?"

Of the 279 replies summarized only 90, or 32 percent, revealed that feedback was being sponsored on a planned, official basis by the universities concerned. Feedback was also accomplished, however, by both formal and informal activities as shown in the following table:

FEEDBACK ACTIVITIES OF PROFESSORS WITH OVERSEAS EXPERIENCE AND NUMBER OF TIMES MENTIONED

INFORMAL ACTIVITIES	NUMBER OF TIMES MENTIONED
1. Lectures, films to civic groups, etc.	133
2. Better teaching	96

[32] Proceedings of a Seminar on "University Goals and Responsibilities in Foreign Operations," held at Michigan State University, May 1965 (Washington: American Council on Education, 1965). (Mimeographed.)

[33] Campus Coordinators Conference, Proceedings, p. 4.

3. Broadening or research   30
4. Continued correspondence with persons and institutions overseas   21
5. Exchange of students encouraged   ·   19
6. Personal benefits to family and self   10

FORMAL ACTIVITIES

1. Advising and counseling with foreign students   71
2. University-sponsored lectures and seminars   60
3. Publications   32
4. Assist with special international events   14
5. Aid to foreign visitors   14
6. Assist with orientation programs   13
7. Development of Office of International Activities   8
8. Establishment of area studies   8
9. Assist with Peace Corps training and orientation   6
10. Reports to administrators   5
11. Regular reports on assistance project to all faculty 5
12. Assist in recruiting of overseas staff   4
13. Catalogue of professors in overseas service   3
14. Participate in debriefing period   1

The replies clearly indicate that in those colleges where the focal point of international programs is a central office having broad interests and responsibilities, the faculty expatriate is better informed about the objectives and importance of his university's overseas commitments. Such an office is now generally understood to be, "a place in the university where all its international functions are considered together, so that directions and priorities can be deliberately set."[34] Such a centralized office also can facilitate the provision of opportunities for the expatriate to share his knowledge and experiences with colleagues, students, and others.

At institutions having such a central office, the predominant point of view is more likely to take for granted, as one respondent stated, that "we have major research and teaching responsi-

[34] *The University and World Affairs,* A Report by the Committee on the University and World Affairs, J. L. Morrill, chairman (New York: Ford Foundation, 1960), p. 34.

bilities in the international area, and we cannot satisfactorily meet these responsibilities without foreign experience."

Another respondent commenting on this point said: "The major contribution the university can make is, it seems to me, to engender the kind of atmosphere that encourages its faculty members to participate fully in foreign service and foreign assignments."

This was in decided contrast to many replies from campuses where all foreign programs are handled separately or independently by the various departments. For example, a professor from an institution in this category wrote: "Most Americans are not interested in other countries and except for my own enrichment and education, my overseas experiences have been a waste of time."

Another professor answered the query about his opportunities to share his experiences with the statement: "A big, round goose egg."

Another stated that co-workers, colleagues, and students generally are apathetic as to what his university or any other institution is trying to accomplish in underdeveloped countries.

"I was particularly impressed by the lack of interest on the part of the so-called internationalists at my university," commented one middle-western professor.

Another stated even more acidly, "I should note that no administrator, colleague, or student at any American university of which I am or have been a member has ever shown any interest in my foreign academic experience. . . . I feel that my reading of the situation is not atypical. I have yet to see an institution in this country making vital and constructive use of striking experiences on foreign campuses which its faculty must inevitably bring home."

In some instances expressions of regret at the lack of interest in world affairs were accompanied by constructive suggestions for feedback from foreign programs. For example, one respondent stated: "The opportunity for feedback is distinctly limited at (this) university. Seminars, dialogs, group discussions in areas of art, philosophy, health, economic development, education, and population problems could be a significant stimulus to scholarship and international interest and achievement."

Without encouragement and assistance from the university administration, the faculty expatriate may find it difficult to initiate a "feedback" from his overseas experiences. Comments of several respondents emphasized this point, of which this one is fairly typical: "Once returned from overseas activities, the average faculty member is immediately caught up in the usual pressures of academic demands to such an extent that he has little time to pursue the year or years abroad to proper use."

The faculty expatriate does not always find it easy to penetrate the administrative barrier. Thus, one respondent stated: "I spent six months . . . making a study of teaching techniques . . . in Asia and in Europe, and found it difficult to get even my dean to read my report."

That the faculty expatriate is sensitive to campus opinion of foreign programs was quite evident in the responses summarized. "Unfortunately," one respondent said, "the attitude among my colleagues seems to be that service abroad is a waste of time and not helpful to an individual's professional development." Another commented: "There is indifference on the part of many of our campus colleagues to our involvement in overseas activities. Each person seems to become more and more involved in his own particular field and consequently has very little time to devote to activities not related to his own field."

And it is likely that many respondents would have agreed with this comment: "But the fact that so often the overseas prophet is without honor on his home-town Main Street helps many an American family decide on another tour of duty abroad." [35]

It is unlikely that feedback to the campus will occur on a continuing basis without deliberate planning. This prompted one respondent to say: "Many good things happen informally and spontaneously, but once an activity grows large and complex, it becomes desirable to consciously strive for feedback and continuous information exchange. This probably requires some formalized structure."

[35] Cleveland *et al., The Overseas Americans,* p. 25.

On the other hand, there were differences of opinion as to what feedback is and how it should be accomplished. There was fairly general agreement, however, that faculty members returning from foreign assignments should continue to be involved in the programs with which they had been associated. It was suggested, among other things, that the overseas professional experiences of the university staff should be used in special faculty lecture-ships, preparation of papers in the field, and in advising foreign students from the countries where the faculty members have served.

Only rarely, however, does it appear that these opportunities are being provided to faculty expatriates by universities. Disap-pointment that such is the case was expressed in such terms as these:

"Feedback is only incidental."
"Experiences not used officially."
"Unsuccessful attempts."
"Department heads not interested."
"Disappointed that there has been no feedback."
"No attempt to take advantage of our experiences."
"A great deficiency."
"Soon forgotten."
"Lots of publicity, but no feedback."
"Proper use not made."
"My name is on file; that is all."

One respondent said that feedback was being emphasized at his university, but he was not sure how this was being accomplished. In some instances, it appeared that faculty expatriates were expecting the university to assume full responsibility for the feedback from their overseas experiences. Yet there were a few who insisted that feedback was an individual responsibility that could best be accomplished by the staff member in his own teaching and research.

One faculty expatriate developed his own feedback program through a new research project. One university with long and varied experience in the international field encourages active programs of teaching and research related to economic development in foreign areas.

Some respondents felt that feedback to the university is a departmental matter, not a university-wide responsibility. But even so, doubt was expressed about the feasibility of modifying highly specialized technical courses in an attempt to benefit students through a feedback from unrelated experiences in foreign countries. On the other hand, it was recognized that the faculty expatriate teaching in a highly technical field might contribute in other ways to the international dimension of his university if he were given an opportunity to do so.

Many respondents expressed gratitude for the opportunities they have had to relate their experiences and to show pictures they had taken to civic and other groups. It is perhaps significant that at this stage in the development of international education programs such opportunities are the principal feedback from the experiences of most faculty expatriates. Yet faculty expatriates themselves recognize that this kind of feedback has much more entertainment than educational value and significance.

Some faculty expatriates have no interest in feedback from experiences in another country and many even speak disparagingly about it. One respondent reacted thus: "There has been no greater opportunity to share whatever knowledge I may have gained than there has been desire on my part to fashion such an opportunity. . . . I might add that I have a kind of vague impression that those who do speak out with authority are likely to be of the 'biddy' variety—those who own a camera (which I don't), join a tour, and 'snap' their way through country after country, thus contributing immensely to the foreigner's idea of the American abroad. Always with something on his docket, a serious scholar continues at work, stopping, perhaps, only to exchange information about study abroad with another scholar digging in the same soil."

Desire for a Continuing Role in International Programs

Replies of those who fit our definition of faculty expatriate revealed a general desire to have a continuing relationship with international programs. Suggestions as to how this might be done most effectively varied considerably. At one university, consideration is being given to the organization of the foreign service personnel group into a seminar to present periodically an open forum for university students and faculty. Yet, more than an occasional seminar is needed to fulfil this desire for a continuing relationship with international programs. Many staff members are disappointed that they are not being consulted or even kept informed about the programs with which they were associated overseas. They find it difficult to understand why they are not asked to participate, even informally, in evaluations of or surveys concerning these programs. In too many instances the campus coordinator or other person having similar on-campus program responsibilities seems reluctant to call on the expatriate faculty to assist with the recruitment and the orientation of new team members or with the counseling of participants and students.

These comments are typical of the views expressed by many respondents:

"I feel strongly that more opportunities should be given to returning personnel to discuss with resident staff members the problems encountered overseas and particularly the training needs of foreign students on our campus."

"It seems to me that every participant in this type of program should be given opportunity to evaluate and criticize the program with which he has been involved. This probably should take place at the end of a tour or on termination of duty."

"My personal recommendation would be that returning staff members be retained on the staff of the International Programs Office on an advisory basis for a period of time. . . . To make better use of individuals with overseas experience requires a level of commitment by the university administration which has not been evident up to the present time."

"Send the most highly qualified person you have . . . then utilize his new experience when he returns."

"Faculty members returning from foreign assignments should have an opportunity to make recommendations regarding the work at the foreign post as well as for international programs on the campus."

"We are attempting to structure our overseas programs in such a way that they will have specific and meaningful relationships with the departments and divisions of the university. . . . It is only through the long-term involvement of our universities in international programs that we will be able to build a corps of internationally conscious and capable staff so that these programs will finally be looked upon as truly being a part of the total commitment of the university."

Several respondents commented that a national directory of professors with overseas interests and experience would be useful in the building of such a corps of internationally oriented university personnel. Such a directory should be an asset in the files of any university whether it has programs overseas or whether its international interests are confined to curricula and special events at home. A few universities already have done this. For example, the University of Minnesota compiled a directory of faculty with international interests in cooperation with its bureau of institutional research in 1964. It contains brief descriptions of the activities and interests of faculty members which are related in some respect to the broad field of international and foreign area studies, and includes teaching, research, and administrative faculty of academic rank from all disciplines. This publication is part of a larger project of Minnesota's Office of International Programs involving a survey of faculty resources in the international field with the objectives of securing accurate indications of faculty capabilities, facilitating communication among faculty members, and increasing cooperation among the various university units in planning, implementation, and assessment of multidisciplinary projects in the international field. The 664 names in the directory represent approximately 40 percent of the university's faculty of academic rank.[36]

[36] Faculty Directory, "International and Foreign Area Interests" (Minneapolis: University of Minnesota, 1964).

Proposals for Campus-Wide Involvement

It has been suggested that "a university might well create within its existing academic and administrative structure a center dealing with the rural sector of the foreign country where the university is giving technical assistance under a contract with the Agency for International Development. . . . For the first semester after returning from an overseas assignment, a staff member might devote a specified portion of his time to duties directly related to his work in the foreign country. This would be a useful transition to regular, full-time staff duties, and, at the same time, contribute significantly to the continuing orientation and preparation of other staff members for similar team assignments overseas." [37]

This arrangement was envisioned as a possible means of developing new area study programs and of coordinating existing area study programs with technical assistance to these areas under AID contracts. In either case, it was felt that better use would be made of returning staff members.

The feasibility of such an arrangement was questioned, however, at a seminar sponsored by the American Council on Education at Michigan State University in May 1965. Views expressed were summarized in the seminar report:

> The point was also made that the individual institution must utilize what resources it has to develop feedback. A small project can serve as a basis for a study program of the area involved. The new AID contract, allowing research, and the use of graduate students in research, enhances the opportunities.
>
> A general discussion followed on development projects and area studies, how they do and do not relate. Ideas were explored on the possibility of feedback from the one to the other. Can centers be created, or the NDEA Language and Area Studies Centers be used, to mesh these two aspects of international activities? It was suggested that the NDEA centers have revealed some basic problems. First,

[37] Arthur D. Weber, "The Role of American Universities in Future Technical Assistance Programs of the Agency for International Development." Paper presented at the Annual Conference of Campus Coordinators AID-India Agricultural Research and Education Program, Ohio State University, Columbus, August 1964. (Mimeographed.)

there is no reason that two scholars interested in one country but in different disciplines should share any common interests. It is not surprising that area studies do not provide a focus for technical assistance. Persons interested in language and literature may be totally uninterested in development.

The very fact that the international office is set apart on campus indicates the difficulty of integrating overseas operations with other campus activities. The label international is exclusive.[38]

While these reservations perhaps are valid for larger universities having well-established area study programs, it would seem that they may not be so for universities without area studies but with AID overseas contracts for technical assistance in developing countries. It could well be that a center dealing with the rural sector of the foreign country where the university is giving technical assistance under an AID contract program would provide the required impetus and the incentive for scholarly area studies not directly related to technical assistance as such. It is conceivable, too, that even such scholarly studies might possibly provide leads to more fruitful avenues of technical assistance.

In any case, the overall objective of the study center concerned with the country where technical assistance is being given probably should be to add to the knowledge and the understanding of international rural development and world affairs by the university community and the citizenry of the state. The original proposal for such a center envisioned that integrated, interdisciplinary research would be conducted on problems affecting the development of the region or country covered by the contract.[39] University staff members would supervise graduate research programs financed under the contract and directed toward the attainment of this objective.

Research projects of both American and foreign graduate students could be related to the rural development problems of the foreign country. Participants from the foreign university would take advanced courses at the American university and

---

[38] "University Goals and Responsibilities in Foreign Operations," p. 19.

[39] Weber, "The Role of American Universities in Future Technical Assistance Programs," p. 7.

develop a research project outline for their thesis problems. Staff members with experience in the foreign country could serve as advisors or in some other capacity in connection with the graduate study program. Actual research on the problems in many instances could be conducted in the students' home countries under the direction of members of university technical assistance teams.

Other objectives of the program ultimately could be:

1. to train agricultural scientists and administrators for careers in international rural development;
2. to conduct campus-based research on key problems of the foreign country or region.

Graduate courses on rural economic development would support and strengthen the research program. Similarly, a limited number of undergraduate courses on foreign and international agricultural would be useful in broadening the training of students who might be attracted to foreign service.

Other suggestions for the on-campus program of such a center include adult education courses, seminars, workshops, and supervised study for individuals and groups from foreign countries, U.S. government agencies, foundations, and private business. In this activity as in the others just mentioned, staff members with overseas experience could have key roles.[40]

As Wharton pointed out recently,[41] Senate Bill S.1212 introduced in the 89th Congress by Senator George McGovern is evidence of increasing interest in promoting more effective international development by utilizing college and university resources. If a university program were established as authorized by this bill, it should be possible to make more effective use of the experiences of staff members after they return from overseas assignments.

In a study by King and Driver respondents were invited to

[40] *Ibid.*, pp. 8-9.

[41] Clifton R. Wharton, Jr., "Revolutionizing Higher Education in the Developing World: Observations on Southeast Asia" (Agricultural Development Council, New York, May 1965). (Mimeographed.)

"state in their own words how their work overseas had carried over to their professional role since returning home."[42]

A wide variety of replies were classified and reported as follows:

> Enhanced teaching—22% of the replies
>
> Publications—15%
>
> General professional competence—36%
>
> Miscellaneous effects such as outside lecturing, correspondence with host colleagues, etc.—26%

The authors noted that "persons who stressed publications as a form of carry-over were, to a disproportionate degree, drawn from the humanities, were supported by Fulbright and Smith-Mundt grants, and proved to be pure teachers in their domestic and in their overseas roles. . . . Fulbrighters tended to be over-represented by the humanities, and people in both these categories tended to play the role of the pure teacher abroad, a role which largely describes their professional activities before leaving home. Returning to the relationship between carry-over and discipline, respondents who benefited in general professional competence were largely natural scientists (only one of whom mentioned publications) and agriculturists (none of whom mentioned publications). Only the social scientists stood out in responding that enhanced teaching had proved an increment. . . . The relationship between carry-over and world regions to which people went for overseas work may be summed up very briefly: For enhancement of teaching and also production of publications, Europe was the most fruitful region and Asia the least rewarding."[43]

Summary and Conclusions

The term *faculty expatriate* is used in this paper to differentiate the university staff member who is serving or has served overseas

---

[42] C. Wendell King and Edwin D. Driver, "Report on a Retrieval Study of the Professional Person Overseas" (Department of Sociology and Anthropology, University of Massachusetts, Amherst, July 1964), p. 41.

[43] *Ibid.*, p. 42.

from the one who has not had such experience. Cognizance is taken of the effects of overseas service on the individual and his university and the reasons for these effects.

Consideration also is given to improving and strengthening the faculty expatriate's contributions to academic programs and the university community. Information on how to accomplish this objective was obtained from replies of faculty expatriates to questions concerning orientation for foreign service and feedback to the campus from their overseas experiences and the programs with which they had been associated.

There is a growing tendency to hold faculty expatriates in higher esteem now that international education and world affairs are receiving greater emphasis at colleges and universities. Previously, a feeling had developed in university circles that persons seeking overseas assignments were likely to be misfits or failures. It was often assumed that the faculty expatriate was either an adventurer seeking thrills or a malcontent hoping to escape from his worries and frustrations. In any case, his professional competence, as well as his motives and objectives, was likely to be questioned by his peers.

In some instances, the overseas performance of the faculty expatriate seemed to justify expressions of doubt about his competence and motives. Of course, rare instances of alleged personal misconduct and moral turpitude received more attention and wider publicity than his other shortcomings. It was not surprising, therefore, that the ugly stereotype thus created sometimes brought ridicule, not praise, for overseas service.

University administrators who have been unwilling to release their best staff members for foreign assignments may have contributed to this unfavorable impression of the faculty expatriate. And comments, facetious or otherwise, about solving a personnel problem by sending a staff member overseas could have had a similar effect. As a consequence, some qualified staff members who otherwise might have volunteered for overseas service have been reluctant to do so; they did not want to be regarded as exiles.

But now that international education and world affairs are providing a new dimension for higher education, the image of the faculty expatriate has improved on most university campuses. Colleges and universities now seldom measure the effect of overseas service in terms of the opportunities provided to get rid of weaker staff members. Yet they often find it difficult to spare enough qualified personnel to staff university-sponsored overseas projects and programs. Indeed, with burgeoning enrollments and rapidly expanding research programs, many higher institutions are hard pressed to meet growing staff requirements on their own campuses.

This new emphasis on international education and world affairs also has serious implications for the competent, conscientious faculty member who accepts an assignment in a foreign country. Unless his work overseas is closely related to and integrated with his regular teaching and research programs, he may not keep in touch with the latest developments in his field. As a consequence, both he and his university are likely to lose, not gain, from his overseas experiences unless program planning and special orientation are provided to prepare and equip him for what he is to do after he returns as well as for his duties while he is away from the university. Thus, part of his foreign assignment should be to anticipate and prepare for his reentry into regular academic duties and affairs. The objective should be to increase the faculty expatriate's contribution to academic programs and the university community through meritorious work and service abroad.

Universities have scarcely made a beginning in developing orientation programs for foreign service. Only 53 percent of 279 faculty members with at least one year's experience overseas reported that they had received orientation for their assignments. Moreover, their comments indicated that orientation relating to their duties and responsibilities abroad was grossly inadequate. Equally disturbing was the fact that not a single respondent mentioned that the orientation program was designed to prepare him to use his overseas experiences after he returned. And when orientation was provided, only administrative procedures and matters concerned with health and travel were covered adequately.

Since orientation for foreign service is either inadequate or not being provided at all, it is not surprising that feedback to the university from overseas experiences and projects has received little attention until recently. Only 32 percent of the 279 respondents referred to above stated that feedback was being sponsored on a planned, official basis by their institutions.

It is not an easy matter to develop and conduct an adequate orientation program for foreign service which will also lead to effective feedback to the campus from overseas experiences and projects. In fact, to provide the briefing needed on a country's culture, history, politics, religion, educational system, development pattern, and national psychology is a task calling for university-wide cooperation and participation. And once the complexity of the orientation process has been recognized and taken into account in the program provided, the logical next step is to involve the entire university in feedback activities. It is unlikely that feedback to the campus will occur on a continuing basis without deliberate planning. Moreover, the faculty expatriate's performance during and after his absence from the campus reflects the overall university commitment and dedication to the international dimension of higher education.

When the entire university community is genuinely interested in and concerned about world affairs and international education, the efforts and accomplishments of the faculty expatriate will be applauded. And, eventually, in such an environment, so many faculty members will have served overseas in some capacity and will have become so deeply committed personally to international education, that the term *faculty expatriate* will no longer be used as the title of an article such as this.

Ralph Smuckler

University Responsibilities
and International
Development Research

One cannot emphasize too strongly the role that systematic study, analysis, and experimentation must play in the evolution of improved methods of development assistance. We have a lot to learn. Research should address itself not only to discovery of new knowledge, but to the devising, designing, and testing of new procedures and materials in technical cooperation, and to the analytical study—for purposes of improved decision-making—of development assistance activities and their consequences.

This statement by John Gardner in his report, *AID and the Universities*,[1] ought to be taken seriously by both sides of the "partnership"—the Agency for International Development and the university community. Both have a research task ahead which requires imaginative talent, energy, and sustained attention. We do, indeed, have "a lot to learn" about the substance and processes of change and development with which we are so concerned.

In the past we have had to plunge into development tasks on a trial-and-error basis. It is not to our credit that we are still frequently doing so. The hard-gained knowledge of one generation of "overseasmen" is diluted in the changeover to another. It is only partial consolation to realize that the lessons of experience

[1] John W. Gardner, *AID and the Universities*, Report from Education and World Affairs in Cooperation with the Agency for International Development (New York: Education and World Affairs, 1964), p. 18.

110

are now becoming better recorded and transmitted than ten years ago, for we still have a long way to go and much to discover.

Systematic research in fields and on problems related to technical assistance has expanded over the past ten years, but it is still very inadequate. As Gardner puts it:

> The most important single fact about development research today is that there isn't enough of it. If it were increased by a factor of ten it would be a more appropriate response to the challenge of development.[2]

Several AID actions in recent years in support of research on development processes are encouraging. The agency's creation of a research division and program is a major beginning step. The inclusion of a research clause in the 1965 revision of the standard university technical assistance contract acknowledges the potential research contribution of contracting universities.

The response of the university community should be enthusiastically supportive. To state the case even more strongly, universities and university people must now exercise initiative and imagination in expanding fundamental and usable knowledge in the development field.

What are some of the questions for which we should now systematically seek answers? What are the priorities? What are some of the avenues now open to research-minded scholars? What is now being done? What problems do we face? These are some of the questions with which this paper is concerned. It cannot present answers in a definitive or final sense, for such an attempt on the part of any one person would be presumptuous; but perhaps the systematic presentation of part of some of the answers will stimulate thought and provoke useful discussion.

Research Needs

We need to know vastly more about many subjects which relate closely to development. Our many and diverse needs can be grouped in four categories:

[2] *Ibid.*, p. 20.

1. Studies of technical assistance administration and programming;

2. Research to facilitate development programming and planning in specific countries or regions;
    3. Research on processes of change and development;
    4. Research leading to technological, scientific, and other innovations applicable to problems of developing areas.

These are not mutually exclusive categories. In complexity they resemble development problems themselves, for most seasoned observers agree the processes and problems of development are not clearcut, neat, or easily separable one from another.

Though we have much to learn we do not start from the very beginning. At the outset, we should recognize that although much must still be uncovered, some scholars have already made a start. Much already is known and written in some fields; and, because of the limits of existing methodology, little of substance can be added through further investigation until we have found new ways of obtaining data. In some fields, highly specialized work must be done on narrowly defined, but crucial matters. But in conducting aid programs and in planning research, it would be as foolish to ignore knowledge which we already have at our disposal, as it would be to restrict all action until research has run its full course and found "all" of the answers.

No one discipline has a monopoly on research related to development. We tend to go through vogues during which we eagerly turn to the economists or anthropologists or natural scientists to discover the "truths." No one of these disciplines, taken alone, has justified our overblown expectations, although each is contributing significantly. Many fields and approaches will continue to be important as we seek knowledge of development. Furthermore, there are many who maintain that an interdisciplinary or multi-disciplinary approach is needed, since the very nature of the problems is too complex for anyone alone to explain satisfactorily.

Not all of the problems we face can be studied in a systematic and sound manner. Many questions of significance must be answered through exercise of judgment based on definition of values and clarification of goals. For these questions, research can be of help, but cannot provide final answers.

Category I: Research on Technical Assistance Administration and Programming. Although we have been engaged in international assistance programs for many years, there are still many unanswered questions about how best to administer, organize, staff, and evaluate these efforts. If this were not true of aid programming, it would be the great exception in the range of human endeavor. However, clarifying studies and research in this instance may be even more important than in other programs. The great importance of the aid program and its sensitive and vulnerable nature demand that we constantly improve its operation, and research studies can contribute some of the answers.

In this first category are research undertakings which deal with questions of administration and operation of technical assistance and aid projects and programs, university efforts included. We now have available a number of studies which help to clarify the important questions and provide some of the answers on matters of suitability of personnel, evaluation of project success, and suitability of various ways of administering technical assistance and aid. We must continue to study these and other important matters.

Studies of Americans working overseas have included intensive examination of narrow aspects of cross-cultural adjustment, broad reviews of predeparture training experience, and studies of the impact of overseas experience on domestic professional careers. In the late 1950's, a major systematic study of overseas American personnel was conducted by the Maxwell School of Citizenship and Public Affairs of Syracuse University. The object of the study was to "reach for suggestive answers to four main questions about Americans abroad:"

- What elements in the education and experience of an American are most relevant to his effective performance on an overseas assignment? (Or, in the question's simplest form: What is so different about living and working abroad?)

- To what extent are these elements central to the education and training processes to which present and prospective overseas Americans are exposed?
- What is now being done to prepare American civilians for overseas service?
- What should the American educational system—and some of its financial sponsors in business, government, and private foundations—be doing in this field? [3]

Analysis of statistics, previous studies, and extensive interview responses yielded much useful information and pointed to five elements of effective overseas performance: technical skill, belief in mission, cultural empathy, a sense for politics, and organization ability. The authors also propose an agenda for action which all universities should study before embarking on training and educational programs for international service.

In a 1963 study, Francis C. Byrnes, through lengthy interviews, took a careful look at thirty-four former technical assistance specialists and analyzed their conceptions of their role overseas.[4]

In studies soon to be published, researchers at the University of Southern California, Pennsylvania State University, the University of Massachusetts, and Massachusetts Institute of Technology have looked at overseas personnel experience from several perspectives. These studies were financed by the Ford Foundation in a coordinated attempt to learn more about career and professional development problems for personnel engaged in international development assignments.[5]

There are also descriptions and analyses of individual agency

[3] Harlan Cleveland, Gerard Mangone, and John C. Adams, *The Overseas Americans* (New York: McGraw-Hill Book Company, 1960), p. vii.

[4] *Americans in Technical Assistance* (New York: Frederick A. Praeger, 1965).

[5] There have been many studies and analyses dealing with recruitment, selection, and evaluation of personnel for development activities including, to mention a few: L. T. Kroeger *et al., Personnel for the Mutual Security Program,* Study No. 2, U. S. Senate, Special Committee to Study the Foreign Aid Program, 1957; Karl Mathieson and Edith Lord, "Report and Recommendations of the Task Force on Recruitment, Screening, and Selection for the Agency for International Development," March 19, 1962 (mimeographed); Mattram Torre, "Personality Adjustment in Overseas Service" in Cleveland and Mangone (eds.), *The Art of Overseasmanship* (Syracuse: Syracuse University Press, 1957).

training programs such as those of the army, AID, universities, and the Department of State. Clarence E. Thurber studied and compared a number of orientation, predeparture, and other training programs and found a wide range of experimentation among universities and government agencies.[6]

Writers and researchers have also been concerned with criteria for evaluation of individual performance, a difficult task at best. Hollis W. Peter and Edwin R. Henry, after reviewing a number of studies in this area, suggest a number of illustrative possibilities: supervisor's ratings, the individual's self-appraisal, evaluation by host country nationals, judgment of outside experts, longevity on the job, objective measures of results or productivity. They conclude that, "the problem of weighing and combining several criterion measures into one measure of job success as a whole is still far from solution." They go on to consider some of the variables which may predict success overseas: personal history, critical incidents, language learning readiness, success in training, ability, and intelligence.[7]

One interesting approach to research on cross-cultural adjustment is suggested by Eugene H. Jacobson in an article on "sojourn research."[8] He divides the overseas experience of the individual into a series of nine phases and considers appropriate research for each. Throughout the sequence, three comparative research threads may be pursued: "Comparative studies of personality, culture, and sojourn maturity." Research on cross-cultural adjustment, including "culture shock," has obvious relevance to problems of personnel effectiveness.

These are some of the serious studies and analyses of overseas personnel which are now in the literature. There are many more,

[6] "The Problem of Training Americans for Service Abroad in U.S. Government Technical Cooperation Programs" (unpublished Ph.D. dissertation, Stanford University, 1961).

[7] "Measuring Successful Performance Overseas," *International Development Review,* III (October 1961), 8-12.

[8] "Sojourn Research: A Definition of the Field," *Journal of Social Issues,* XIX, No. 3 (July 1963). This entire issue of the journal is devoted to "Human Factors in Cross-Cultural Adjustment" and contains a number of useful articles and reports on research.

and there are other studies in process; but there is still much to be learned in this one segment of important knowledge related to how we can operate more effectively abroad.

For some time, universities have been trying to estimate and evaluate the impact of technical assistance and exchange programs on the countries within which they are working overseas. Reciprocally, they seek to understand the impact of overseas programs on their own home campuses. In a study financed by the Carnegie Corporation, Edward W. Weidner and associates at Michigan State University undertook to measure these two-way effects. Just as the study by Harlan Cleveland and associates is "must" reading for those university people studying overseas personnel, the studies by Weidner and colleagues should be read by those concerned with the world role of universities.[9] Not that further research in these two areas is not needed; but both represent major efforts which add much and should be considered as basic to further examination.

Research by university personnel is but one of many approaches to study of development problems. Various other approaches, which, perhaps, are more direct, have been examined and still need further analysis. The National Planning Association project on technical cooperation in Latin America begun in 1953 resulted in a number of major studies and publications. These were financed by the Ford Foundation and provide an excellent beginning point for those concerned with the variety of approaches to technical cooperation in Latin America. One ap-

[9] *The World Role of Universities* (New York: McGraw Hill Book Company, 1962). This is the summary volume of the series. Others are: Weidner *et al., The International Programs of American Universities* (East Lansing: Institute of Research on Overseas Programs, 1958); Martin Bronfenbrenner, *Academic Encounter: The American University in Japan and Korea* (New York: The Macmillan Company, 1961); Henry Hart, *Campus India, An Appraisal of American College Programs in India* (East Lansing: Michigan State University Press, 1961); Richard N. Adams and Charles C. Cumberland, *United States University Cooperation in Latin America* (East Lansing: Institute of Research on Overseas Programs, 1960); Walter Adams and John A. Garraty, *Is the World Our Campus?* (East Lansing: Michigan State University Press, 1960); Bruce L. Smith, *Indonesian-American Cooperation in Higher Education* (East Lansing: Institute of Research on Overseas Programs, 1960).

proach, that of the "servicio," is thoroughly considered in the study in this series by Philip M. Glick.[10]

Other studies analyze and evaluate the work in Taiwan of the Joint Commission for Rural Reconstruction as another way of administering development assistance in another part of the world.[11] Multi-national efforts, such as the Colombo Plan, and efforts by international agencies have also been studied. The Russian and Chinese aid programs have been described. And certainly the organization and administration of the U. S. aid program has been observed, studied, dissected, analyzed, criticized, and praised in its total form and in subsections.

But in spite of all this we still need to seek through research to find better ways to assist development, for many questions still go unanswered. We are still seeking to evaluate overseas development projects more sharply, more objectively, more intelligently.[12]

Evaluation, though necessary, can be a very difficult task. Criteria are frequently ill-defined; and objective and accurate methods of measuring success are lacking or ill-suited. Furthermore, too frequently, evaluation research is done too soon or too rapidly and lacks perspective over time. Clearly much needs to be done to clarify criteria and methods of evaluation. Poorly done evaluation studies can do more harm than good, especially if they focus on the spectacular and flamboyant.

Perhaps the most useful writing on this subject can be found in a UNESCO publication, *Measuring the Results of Develop-*

[10] *The Administration of Technical Assistance* (Chicago: University of Chicago Press, 1957). Others in the series: Arthur T. Mosher, *Technical Cooperation in Latin America* and James G. Maddox, *Technical Assistance by Religious Agencies in Latin America.*

[11] Annual reports of the Joint Commission for Rural Reconstruction are useful in reviewing its work over the years. See also: *A Decade of Rural Progress, 1948-1958* (Taipei: Joint Commission for Rural Reconstruction, 1958); A. F. Raper, *Rural Taiwan—Problem and Promise* (Taipei: Joint Commission for Rural Reconstruction, 1953); E. S. Kirby, *Rural Progress in Taiwan* (Taipei: Joint Commission for Rural Reconstruction, 1960).

[12] A new study to evaluate university institution-building efforts in agriculture is being carried out by the Committee on Institutional Cooperation (C.I.C.) with AID sponsorship. AID is also supporting a study of technical assistance administration in agriculture being done by the Maxwell School of Syracuse University.

ment Projects by Samuel P. Hayes, Jr.[13] Hayes suggests four steps to the complicated task of identifying and measuring changes resulting from a development project:

1. Describe the development project and specify its goals;
2. Decide what data to use to indicate project results;
3. Compile and collect these data—before, during, and after;
4. Analyze and interpret the findings, and review them with interested groups.

Hayes points out that: "Uncovering the results of individual projects is simpler and less costly (than analyzing whole programs) and can often be carried on by the persons directly involved in the project." [14] If universities and others engaged in projects abroad would heed his suggestion, we would be amassing far more useful and accurate data with which to measure progress, and to evaluate project success or failure.

Category II: Research to Facilitate Development Programming and Planning in Specific Countries or Regions. In a sense, all research which tells us more about how to administer aid programs or adds to our understanding of development processes, also facilitates development programming and planning. But there are some studies to be made which essentially describe and analyze local conditions and which are directly applicable and necessary for intelligent programming of aid resources and planning of development. Without description, basic data compilation, and thoughtful analysis of relationships, planning would be wasted and resources would be poorly allocated.

A number of studies are now under way in Africa which illustrate this type of essential research. In Spring 1964, AID requested a study and analysis of training opportunities available to Africans within their home countries and in third-country locations. The study, which covered a number of African coun-

---

[13] UNESCO, 1959. This "manual for the use of field workers" was prepared as the first UNESCO monograph in the applied social sciences.

[14] *Ibid.,* pp. 15-16.

tries, also analyzed projections of manpower needs and educational development plans. The main purpose of the study from AID's standpoint was to enable it to plan and administer its participant training program and related activities more prudently.[15]

Two studies now under way in Nigeria under AID auspices provide further illustrations. One is an assessment of educational development needs and plans in relation to manpower projections; a second study is concerned with agricultural and rural development. The former is being done by a committee of Education and World Affairs; the latter, by an *ad hoc* consortium of universities working under AID contracts in the field of agriculture in Nigeria (Michigan State, Wisconsin, Kansas State, and Colorado State). Both are expected to yield information and insight which will facilitate wise use of aid program funds and energy.

In 1963, the American International Association for Economic and Social Development (A.I.A.) studied the agricultural and settlement potential of the "Planalto Central" of Brazil.[16] The product, a comprehensive, interdisciplinary survey, was presented to the sponsor of the study, AID, and will serve as a basis for future programs in that vast area. It identified a need for more intensive and specialized investigations. The A.I.A. survey is another of many examples of this category of research, which can be identified within any one country or region.

There is an unending need for studies of this type. Included generally would be manpower studies, industry feasibility studies, crop surveys, administrative and social organization descriptions, surveys of school systems, cost analyses of many varieties, soil and other natural resource surveys, and many others. In many cases, all that is needed is a pulling together and systematizing of existing data and studies. Universities can play an important role in this type of much needed research.

[15] The study was undertaken by Education and World Affairs in cooperation with the African Liaison Committee of the American Council on Education. John Masland was study director. Findings are to be published.

[16] Walter L. Crawford *et al., Survey of the Agricultural Potential of the Central Plateau of Brazil* (New York: American International Association, 1963).

Category III: Research on Development and Change Processes. What are the crucial processes through which "modernization" occurs in a given society? How can change be induced successfully in various cultures? Anthropologists, sociologists, political scientists, economists, and many others have been at work on answers to various components of these broad questions. The need for research in this fundamental area is as endless as change itself. We need to get more of our best social science researchers interested in questions relating to the processes of change and development.

To illustrate gains which are being made, of several broad research efforts now under way one major effort is an attempt to determine the importance of certain variables in the process of building new institutions abroad, a process in which many universities are now involved. A group of universities with headquarters at the University of Pittsburgh (co-sponsored by researchers at Indiana, Syracuse, and Michigan State) has started a number of studies in this direction. For this research, "institution-building" has been defined as "the planning, structuring, and guidance of new or reconstituted organizations which (a) embody changes in values, functions, and/or technologies, (b) establish, foster, and protect new normative relationships and action patterns, and (c) attain support and complementarity in the environment." Examples of such institutions are development banks, planning agencies, and universities.

A number of central concepts have been formulated to guide the research in its early stages. Among these are clusters of variables pertaining to the institution as a social system, variables related to leadership, doctrine, program, resources, and internal structure. Within each of the clusters, a number of elements and properties have been identified which appear significant for the analysis of the institution-building process. The analytical framework also includes the concept of institutional linkages, points of interaction with the environment. These linkages are grouped into various classes.[17]

---

[17] See *Inter-University Research Program in Institution-Building* and other explanatory materials available through the Graduate School of Public and Inter-

This framework of institution-building analysis is now being applied through research on university development in Ecuador, on a College of Education in Nigeria, on an Institute of Public Administration in Thailand, and on a civil service staff training academy in Pakistan. These studies will be comparable and over the years many such studies will contribute similar data within these analytical categories. This represents a careful, systematic approach within an analytical framework which will be adjusted and modified as research indicates a need. Ultimately, research such as this could be of great value practically as well as theoretically. It could lead us to a more fundamental understanding of what we are engaged in and to more effective institution-building efforts overseas.[18]

Another important new study is concerned with accelerating the diffusion and adoption of modern agricultural technology under a wide range of social and economic conditions in developing countries. The study seeks to learn which communication channels and techniques are most effective under varying social and cultural conditions. Its findings should provide useful guidelines for action programs. The study will focus on Brazil, Nigeria, and India.[19]

Any examples of social science research related to development processes would only be minimally illustrative. Within each discipline—anthropology, sociology, psychology, political science, and economics—there are many studies and groups of scholars concerned with research problems which are relevant to the international development field. Within political science for example, the work of the Committee on Comparative Politics of the Social Science Research Council is providing an analytical

---

national Affairs, University of Pittsburgh. Main support for the inter-university program comes from a Ford Foundation grant. AID is also supporting part of the research.

[18] A bibliography recently circulated by the institution-building research program contained several hundred relevant entries.

[19] The study will be directed by Professor Everett Rogers in the Department of Communication and the International Communications Institute at Michigan State University. An AID contract supports the study.

framework and a series of individual studies related to political development.[20] The Comparative Administration Group (C.A.G.) of the American Society for Public Administration includes scholars contributing to knowledge of the conduct of development efforts; i.e., the administration of development programs. From their work have come a large number of thoughtful papers, several studies, and a number of suggestive and potentially productive avenues for research on development administration.[21]

Much has been done by these social science researchers, but much more is needed. Many of the tasks of development can proceed only with a full knowledge and understanding of the behavior of people. It is not enough to know that a wheat crop could be doubled by using certain amounts of chemical fertilizer at specified intervals. We must also know the economic cost of the fertilizer, its comparative economic value as an innovation in terms of market value of the new product, and other factors. We must know how to make the administrative and communication systems work so that the information leading to adoption of the innovation can be reasonably effective and so that the crop can find its way to a good market. We have to know the behavior of the peasant, his willingness to accept change under various circumstances. We should know the social effects of increased family income from the larger wheat crop. And we must balance all of this within an expanded knowledge of political impact and governmental change. To know that the fertilizer—or irrigation, or some other innovation—will "work" is not enough. University

[20] See G. Almond and J. Coleman (eds.), *The Politics of the Developing Areas* (Princeton: Princeton University Press, 1960); Robert E. Ward and Dankwart A. Rustow, *Political Modernization in Japan and Turkey* (Princeton: Princeton University Press, 1964); Lucian W. Pye (ed.), *Communications and Political Development* (Princeton: Princeton University Press, 1963); and J. LaPalombara (ed.), *Bureaucracy and Political Development* (Princeton: Princeton University Press, 1963).

[21] See Edward W. Weidner and A. Spitz, *Development Administration, An Annotated Bibliography* (Honolulu: East-West Center Press, 1963); also various publications of the C.A.G. as listed in the *C.A.G. Newsletter*, III, No. 2 (February 1965). The C.A.G. with headquarters at the University of Indiana is led by Professor Fred Riggs.

researchers of the highest competence must be encouraged to find answers to these many other crucial questions.[22]

Category IV: Research Leading to Technical and Scientific Innovation. Within this fourth category we can include the vital contributions made by scientists and those in applied scientific fields. It is frequently suggested that we know enough already to satisfy needs of developing areas but must concentrate now on finding ways to extend knowledge to the many. One can also point to signs that this often heard generalization is only partially true. Do we know enough about rice, the main crop which sustains so many millions in Asia? What about various parasites including those carried by the tsetse fly which make it so difficult to raise livestock in parts of Africa? There is still scientific work to be done on birth control, on new uses for old crops, on water control and use, on desalinization, on tropical diseases, on nutritional problems, on fertilizers, on the use of solar energy, and on many other matters which should continue to challenge scientists for many generations.

AID is now supporting a number of studies in the field of agriculture which illustrate the types of research needed. Basic research on the nutritional status of soils in Latin America is now under way by scientists at North Carolina State University. Latin America must double agricultural output in the next twenty years in order to increase per capita food supply. This research project will be directed toward a major factor related to expanded crop productivity.

Another study is directed toward development and use of improved varieties of major cereal crops in Africa.

A third research endeavor deals with tsetse fly control or eradication through use of the sterility method. Biological methods used successfully against the screw worm in the U. S. are being used experimentally against the tsetse fly in this project centered in Salisbury, Southern Rhodesia.

[22] Research needs were more completely identified by distinguished participants in two meetings, one convened by the Brookings Institution, the other by the International Institute for Educational Planning. See *Development of the Emerging Countries: An Agenda for Research* (Washington: Brookings Institution, 1962) and *Educational Planning: An Inventory of Major Research Needs* (Paris: I.I.E.P., 1964).

Here are titles of some of the agricultural science research projects suggested by AID staff members and others: Desalinization and Salt Control Research on Agricultural Soils of Arid Regions; Improvement of Vegetables in Southeast Asia; Chemisterilants for Noxious Wild Birds; Research on the Eradication of Snails which are Carriers of Schistosomiasis (bilharzia).[23]

These examples are drawn from agriculture, but the needs for research are much broader. The AID research program also suggests studies in public health, engineering, and other technical and scientific fields. For example:

> *Adaptation and Innovation Engineering in Industrial Production:* The adaptation of imported, and the upgrading of local, technology in the industrial system of developing countries is a particularly visible problem in the general process of modernization. The research envisaged would consist of selected engineering studies, both theoretical and experimental, on questions of the following types: (1) the feasibility and the suitability of specific inventions or adaptations of existing technology; (2) engineering identification of industrial production problems in developing economies which present technological challenges; (3) examination of certain promising areas of modern technology from the viewpoint of inventive adaptation to conditions abroad.[24]

The suggestions of AID are by no means definitive or all-inclusive. The boundaries of the needs for research are as broad as science itself. Who can predict the productive research directions which will be followed as we attract our best research minds into these efforts?

Several Approaches to Research by the Universities

The assault on these various categories of research tasks must be made along several routes simultaneously. The need is too great to permit anything less. We must find ways to accelerate

[23] See *AID Research Program in Agriculture and Rural Development, FY 1962-1967* (Washington: Agency for International Development, January 1965).

[24] *Contract Program in Research and Analysis* (Washington: Agency for International Development, Rev. April 7, 1964), p. 9.

the growth of knowledge and its effective application to the problems of developing areas.

One route—support of individual scholars—is traditional, well tested, and known to be useful. We must continue to encourage the individual scholar and groups of researchers who have contributed so much through research in the past. The AID research program must expand its support of worthwhile individual scholarship on problems of development. Other agencies of the government, private foundations, and universities themselves are also potential sources of expanded support for scientific and other studies of immediate and long-range significance in the international field.

Beyond this, however, the AID-university contract system itself could be put to even greater effectiveness in research if universities would expand initiative in this direction.

One university contribution should be the stimulation of research programs within each of the new institutions we are helping to develop overseas. If American universities are to be true to their own tradition, they must insist that the research component be incorporated as a part of the normal, healthy growth of educational institutions in the emerging nations. A strong interest and ability in research on the part of local personnel should be one criterion for deciding whether or not a successful institution-building effort has been realized.

It is true that this research emphasis would be, in some countries, contrary to prior educational tradition; but that should not deter us. By helping to find ways to install strong research programs conducted by indigenous personnel we would be taking a major step toward eventually finding the answers we need. Over the years, we would be much farther ahead.

Furthermore, we would be encouraging a process which could contribute greatly to the quality of the overall educational product of the new institution. Publication derived from studies of matters close to home by local professors—studies, case studies, data compilations and analyses, descriptions—would provide much needed classroom materials rooted in the reality of the local society. Too often and for too long, students in Africa have studied the "flora and fauna" of England or France, and have learned public or business administration through cases drawn from U. S. experience and tied to American institutions.

Finally, building strong indigenous research programs would provide productive research bases for U. S. and other scholars dedicated to examining topics appropriate to the developing areas. Collaborative research would follow, and the quality and relevance of research output by both the western and the non-western research partner would be enhanced.

Another route to the expansion of knowledge is to add a re-search component—perhaps even a research obligation—to many university technical assistance contracts. This addition would have a number of outcomes. First, it would broaden and expand overall research activity and product. Second, it would help to assure that research is done on relevant subjects, i.e., related to the very processes and complexities of development which the university and others are addressing. It might also provide an immediate application of new knowledge, since the research product would be kept close to the potential user. Third, as a by-product it would help attract high quality talent into the university contract program generally.

It is the obligation of universities to insist that the research component in new contracts be carefully—and usually affirma-tively—considered. Once included in the contract, the university must insist that the research effort keep pace with the quality and perserverance of other parts of the specific overseas contract project. Qualified faculty must design and carry out the research; publication of findings must not lag.

Adding a general research component to university technical assistance contracts would not replace the need to establish and support specific additional research projects which would operate independent of institution-building efforts. Some studies could best proceed independently. Some are best pursued in several countries and thus could not be encompassed within a single technical assistance contract.

In some instances, because of the breadth or complexity of the research project AID or other sponsors should be encouraged to seek multi-university groups or consortia to undertake the re-search. An example of this approach is the four university group mentioned above which is studying agricultural potential and planning in Nigeria. In that particular case, all four institutions are also active in agricultural technical assistance work in that country; therefore, there were clear advantages to use their research abilities as well.

The new standard contract recognizes the possibility of making use of graduate students in university projects. Universities ought to see that they are well integrated into the research plans under the contract. Their contribution can be significant. And over the long run, their involvement in serious, systematic overseas re-search will yield an expanded "next generation" of researchers able and eager to build the knowledge base essential to develop-ment programs.

Furthermore, by including a reasonable graduate student com-ponent in overseas project work, universities can more easily interest more capable faculty members in overseas assignment. The problem of disruption in graduate programs could be par-tially solved. The professor who takes with him several advanced graduate students is in a position to multiply the impact of his stay abroad and to contribute in directions not previously possible.

What is needed is university initiative and imaginative leader-ship. The AID endorsement of the Gardner report, the expan-sion of the contract provisions to recognize clearly the possibility of research and the use of graduate students, plus the develop-ment of the new university grants program, open the door. But it remains for the universities to make full use of these oppor-tunities and thus contribute even more positively to develop-ment abroad. Universities should seriously consider this sug-gestion of John Gardner:

> Universities have always seen it as one of their primary responsibilities to create the conditions and circumstances in which their scholars can do creative work. Thus they build and maintain multi-million dollar research libraries, nuclear accelerators, and astronomical observatories. If they face up to their comparable responsibilities in the field of

development, they might create important development research centers on their own campuses and research stations overseas.[25]

Research Problems

We have had enough experience in international development research to permit us to identify some of the problems which we cannot ignore as we expand our efforts. Although the difficulties are great they are not prohibitive. They must be taken into account by the university community and treated as carefully as possible in designing and carrying out research on development.

Certain problems occur because of the nature of the setting itself; others, because of the complex nature of the questions we are trying to answer. Other problems can be traced to the understandable impatience, the over-eagerness of those in development activities.

Nature of Setting

Many of the countries within which research must take place are governed by precarious regimes, are thirsting to realize full equality and rapid social and economic growth, are sensitive to outside (or even internal) criticism, are frequently overloaded with studies and analyses of questionable usefulness, and are undermanned with talent able to carry through development schemes. This type of setting generates research problems.

Immediately, the researcher is faced with the need to exercise extra discretion in using data and publishing conclusions. One cannot assume that a carefully designed and well executed study will yield an immediately publishable manuscript, since publication may result in denying access to future researchers (and others) or in regressive measures by the government in power. This is particularly true in social science studies.

In some countries there is now clear evidence that research which calls for interviewing top officials ought to be limited; not because of sensitivity, but just because too often the process is

---

[25] *AID and the Universities,* p. 20. An excellent example of university-AID collaboration along this line is the Land Tenure Center at the University of Wisconsin.

operating contrary to productivity and efficiency of the government. The same few officials are being interviewed too often. The benefits of the research product are not balancing the loss of time and the nuisance to decision makers. Furthermore, the problem is magnified when the interviewing is by outsiders, some of whom have not explored alternative sources of information or, due to scanty experience or prior study, have not pinpointed the type of questions needed. Everybody wants to talk to the harassed Minister of Education; few will settle for data or answers coming from his subordinates, sufficient as such may be in some cases.

Even when top officials are not involved, outside researchers are wearing out the "welcome mat" in some countries. This has been noticeable in certain African countries and in Latin America. In a sense, the foreign scholar becomes a "carpetbag" researcher unless he has well established relationships and shares his research plans, data, and conclusions with interested local scholars.

There are many operating problems arising out of the nature of the setting: the general inadequacy or lack of important statistical data, the shortage of research assistants and trained interviewers, communications and transportation difficulties, shortage and maintenance problems related to electrical and laboratory equipment. All of these argue for extreme care in designing, scheduling, and controlling research projects. They also suggest the increasing desirability for close collaborative efforts with local scholars and local research organizations. AID and the universities should do all they can to strengthen these joint endeavors.

The damaging experience in research project "Camelot" which recently exploded in Latin America can be drawn on to illustrate many of the problems of international research. Among other things, it points clearly to the need to establish close scholarly relations with colleagues and institutions abroad. However, even then, some problems may not be researchable for reasons of sensitivity.[26]

---

[26] See Kalman H. Silvert, "American Academic Ethics and Social Research Abroad: The Lesson of Project Camelot," *American Universities Field Service* (West Coast South America Series), XII, No. 3, 1-21.

Nature of Research Subjects

Some of the research problems which need attention are manageable without requiring advance in methodology. Some agricultural research, certain health studies, and others in the natural sciences can be transferred, with some adaptation, to the less developed countries. The methods are fairly clear and probably would yield success over time in Africa or India as they have in Iowa or France.

However, for many of the crucial questions related to the processes of change, even in more advanced countries, research cannot yet provide answers. Techniques of data collection and analysis have not yet caught up with the complex nature of the questions raised. The number of variables in some seemingly simple behavioral research problem prohibits conclusive research products even in the advanced countries. In short, limitations on methodology set limits to what we can do in researching many vital problems in this field. The complex nature of the problems we face abroad will require expansion of our research sophistication if we are to find the answers we need.

If we are to proceed we must have far more talented researchers taking a direct interest in research problems abroad. The expansion of research opportunities in more comfortable and established settings at home makes it difficult to attract the quality of talent we need in studies abroad. Although the overseas challenge is great, there are also many interesting research possibilities at home.

Furthermore, research interest and ability is in short supply within underdeveloped countries. Since the research problems are difficult, highly qualified researchers are needed; and they will not be easy to produce. A shortage will be with us for some time.

The only way we will make rapid progress in overcoming these difficulties is to expand the total effort and be sure that we are not wasting resources. As suggested above, research tied to institution-building efforts will help overcome personnel shortages, and also provide a ready market for the research findings.

Another possibility is to buildup and sustain major research facilities abroad. The efforts of the foundations in establishing such major, sustained programs can serve as models. The relatively new Rice Research Institute in the Philippines and the planned Tropical Agriculture Institute in West Africa are good examples. These offer the advantages of continuity and sharpening of focus. They would also provide more attractive settings for U. S. and other researchers to pursue specialized and long-range investigations. Cooperative efforts by universities to exercise initiative along this line are overdue.

Over-Eagerness

For good reasons, the leaders and people of the emerging countries want to attain the fruits of development quickly. Few are willing to think in terms of generations of gradual progress. Most seek sustained, rapid growth.

Although there is bound to be much frustration, it is logical that Americans and others assisting in development must also strive to move the process along quickly and to do whatever they can to satisfy these expectations. We must certainly attempt to bring expectations in line with reality, but if we are to be effective contributors we must help keep the pace as rapid as we can.

Within our own country there has been much short-term thinking as well. Congress has not been willing to consider the aid program as a long-range endeavor. And as a result, in spite of all informed advice to the contrary, we are frequently forced to stress immediate impact research programs and premature termination of institution-building projects.

The difficulties arising are clear. Early impact studies abound. Emphasis on basic research lags; long-term studies are not often projected; inadequate evaluation studies are encouraged. Universities must be sure that their research energies and talent are not wasted on poor research designed to meet inappropriate deadlines in spite of the complexity of the problems. While they must strive to move quickly, they must not assume that speed is always possible or wise.

Our tendency to be caught up in a whirl of time pressure also yields a projection of broad, surface-level research on complex problems where careful analysis calls for piece by piece investigation. For example, we cannot evaluate overall "success and failure" in personnel performance overseas until we have first looked carefully at many components. Nor can we systematically study such broad subjects before criteria are developed and before many other questions depending upon defining goals and values are answered.

Summary

The need for expanded research related to development is abundantly clear. The need for broader initiative by universities and university faculty is great. Expansion of knowledge must accompany application and transmission of knowledge if we are to be true to our university traditions and if we are to be effective in what we are attempting to do overseas.

Research needs can be viewed in four major categories:

1. Studies of technical assistance administration and programming—including research on administration and operation of technical assistance and aid projects, overseas personnel matters, evaluation, etc.

2. Research to facilitate development programming and planning in specific countries—including manpower studies, industry feasibility studies, surveys of school systems, soil and natural resource surveys, various types of data compilations, etc.

3. Research on development and change processes—including social science studies of institution-building, behavioral studies, economic analyses, etc.

4. Research leading to scientific or technical innovation—including studies involving agricultural scientists, public health and medical personnel, engineers and scientists, etc.

Within each category important research is in progress, but there is room for expansion and improvement. Much of the research requires sophisticated methodology and a thorough knowledge of what has been attempted to date. The research tasks are difficult and call for our best efforts, in many cases on a multi- or interdisciplinary basis. Furthermore, not all problems of development call for research; some problems can only be solved by good judgment, weighing of values, and clear statement of goals. While research cannot provide us with answers to all the questions, it can help with many.

In pursuing expanded development research we should try several approaches. First, the support of individual, capable scholars is traditional, productive, and should be continued and expanded. Second, the AID technical assistance contract system should place increasing emphasis on incorporating a research dimension in most AID-university programs. This should include building research activity into the overseas institution as it develops. It should also include adding a research component or obligation into the university contract. This is permitted by the new standard contract as is inclusion of graduate students in the research or related aspects of the contract project. Universities should exercise full initiative to see that these important new possibilities are included regularly in program planning and contract negotiation.

There is no shortage of problems in carrying out research on development overseas. Some problems derive from the nature of the setting, others from the complex nature of the research subjects, and still others from the pressure for speed. None of these are insurmountable, but they do suggest need for extra care, careful strategy and design, close working relationships with local researchers, and a need for new major research centers abroad.

Edward Weidner

Evaluation of the Impact
of University Contracting Abroad

Many have pointed with pride. Others have viewed with alarm. But whatever their opinion, most administrators and professors at American universities have strong views on the effectiveness and appropriateness of university contracting abroad. The lack of consensus does not mark only the universities. Government administrators, foundation executives, and others concerned with higher education or development have also expressed positive feelings, often in different terms.

While this is not an area where there has been general agreement, two generalizations are common. It is frequently reported that universities are "doing better" abroad than they were doing five, ten, or fifteen years ago. The most optimistic and the most pessimistic observer would readily agree that there is a large range covered between the project with the most impact and that with the least (or even a negative) impact.

What, then, accounts for the differences in opinion on the effectiveness of university contracting abroad? What accounts for the project of one institution being generally considered successful and that of another greatly inadequate? Is it true that universities are becoming more skilled and effective abroad?

No attempt at major social innovation elicits a uniform response of appreciation or of evaluation. There is no reason to suppose that in their innovating roles abroad American universities should be any exception. Still, a search for the answers to the questions just presented needs to be treated seriously by aca-

134

demicians and non-academicians alike. The role and effectiveness
of universities both at home and abroad is always of prime importance to the nation.

Evaluation of the overseas impact of university contracting
abroad begins, quite naturally, with an examination of the goals,
aims, and objectives of projects. The conditions which the project
encountered originally, frequently called benchmarks, must be
established, and techniques for measuring or judging change
identified. Results must be assessed and the causes therefore.
Even after all these steps are taken, the assessment of a project
is not complete. Full evaluation requires a comparison of the
success of one project with that of other similar undertakings.
There may even be non-university techniques of securing change
abroad that would be more suitable or more effective. University
contracting overseas should be evaluated in terms of its own
success, the other alternatives available, and the costs and gains
that accrue.

While evaluation of university overseas projects is difficult and
the perfect evaluation undoubtedly beyond reach, there is no
reason to be so discouraged as to give up evaluation studies. The
caveats contained in the present essay are meant as guidelines for
improvement in evaluations as opportunity and resources afford,
not as a set of barriers to prevent their undertaking.

Goals, Aims, and Objectives

Each project abroad has a series of broad goals, intermediate
aims, and specific objectives. At the most general level, the projects may contribute to host country development, to its political,
economic, cultural, and educational growth. They may also contribute to the foreign policy aims of the host country or of the
United States by furthering mutual security, helping combat
communism, strengthening international friendships, and furthering intercourse among different peoples. Contracts overseas may
be a means of advancing man's knowledge about countries or
topics that have not adequately come under systematic inquiry.

The two most common intermediate aims of university projects abroad are institution-building and, ultimately and indirectly through host country personnel who have participated in the project, the education and training of certain portions of the host country population. Those who participate in a project can be termed culture carriers or intermediaries, and those who they in turn contact or who are ultimately affected by the culture impact can, for convenience, be termed target groups. Such aims are intermediate in the sense that they are not directly the activities in which American professors engage while abroad, but they are among the mid-term results of successful work abroad. If the work that is being undertaken is institutionalized before the project ends and if the training of trainers or the educating of educators has been significantly augmented, then institution-building has occurred and target groups will be affected by the existence of the project for years to come. An additional intermediate aim is the strengthening of the American university in regard to its instructional, research, or faculty development program.

At the most specific level of a university project overseas, its objectives are immediately related to the activities in which the American professors engage. A demonstration of teaching techniques, the introduction of a new course, the training of a host country faculty member, the publication of a textbook or the completion of a research project—all represent what the professors may do and are usually the specific objectives detailed in the contract.

Concerning each project, there is a steady progression from the most specific objectives, to the intermediate aims, and on to the most general goals. Thus a project in which professors of chemistry from the United States go to the host country to teach, demonstrate new or more effective teaching techniques, and train host country professors of chemistry may be related to a desire to expand the number of trained chemists available for additional or enlarged local industries and the latter in turn may be related to the economic development of the country. The same chemistry teaching project may be a part of a larger effort to build a new university or a new type of university with a new type of faculty, teaching, and student-faculty relationship which in turn will increase the capacity of the system of higher education of the country and thus contribute to development in all its varied forms.

To the American university, sending professors of chemistry abroad may be a part of a plan to expand the chemistry department somewhat earlier than regular funds would otherwise permit, to enable advanced preparations for an expected increase in students and contribute to the orderly growth of the institution. There may also be great interest in the teaching of science, and the American university may welcome an opportunity to send chemistry professors abroad since additional experience in and research on science teaching will thereby be facilitated, and a significant contribution to man's knowledge made possible.

The United States government may have still another goal. Relations with the host country may be strained, and an American presence difficult to establish. Teaching chemistry may seem rather harmless politically and educationally, and therefore it may be an area in which some intercourse among the two countries can occur. The success of the project from the United States government's point of view may be heavily dependent upon whether American-host country friendship is nourished and additional opportunities for contact developed.

Clarity of Purposes

The evaluation of a project must in the first instance depend upon its goals, aims, and objectives. Unfortunately, some lack of clarity is almost always present in defining them. It is easiest, of course, to obtain agreement on the specific objectives of a project when a contract for assistance is being negotiated. The contract normally lists the major activities in which American university professors will engage while abroad, and each party to the contract can alter the list at will before final agreement is reached. The more detailed contracts may include a list of activities and a list of subjects, such as teaching, demonstrations, and curricular development in public administration, personnel and fiscal management, and human relations. From the standpoint of evaluation, however, even such a list provides a somewhat inadequate set of objectives against which to measure accomplishments. It does not indicate more general purposes, priorities, or the direction curricular development is to take.

In official project documents, there is seldom a detailing of the broad goals underlying a project, except perhaps in purely formal terms, and even the intermediate aims may not be spelled out. Among the middle-level aims, institution-building is commonly mentioned only if a complete new university, school, or agency is to be created. The many less showy aspects of institution-building perforce go unlisted. Target groups—the planned ultimate recipients of knowledge, skills, or other culture items—are seldom mentioned, much less identified in quantitative and qualitative terms. Which government officials need education and training, how many of them are there, and how much training? How can the "spread effect" of a relatively small school of public administration be great enough to encompass a large government ministry or series of ministries, with their tens of thousands of employees?

Where underlying goals are mentioned in contracts or agreements they are frequently included in "whereas" clauses or formal introductory paragraphs, and no attempt is made to relate specific project activities to them or to define them in measurable or operational terms. The goals of economic and social development of the host country will often be mentioned in contracts, but others are not found very frequently.

The listing of objectives, aims, and goals in formal project agreements is thus helpful to the evaluation process, but is not an adequate guide to all project purposes. In the majority of cases, there are reports or memoranda of host country groups, sponsoring organizations, or survey teams that may indicate the circumstances or conditions that gave rise to the project, and may spell out in some detail the objectives and aims that at least some parties wished to achieve. Even though such documents may not have official standing, they are invaluable guides to project purposes, or at least the intention of some of the parties to the agreement at certain points in time.

Almost inevitably, the several groups cooperating in a project will have somewhat different points of emphasis and often their purposes will diverge significantly. An American university team, a host country group, and a financial sponsor such as the Agency for International Development or a foundation may see quite different opportunities presented to them by a project. Even within each of these groups there may be wide variations in the perception of a project. The field team of an American university may be oblivious to the point of view on the home campus, mission headquarters may disagree with Washington, and host country participants may have far different attitudes from those in other parts of their university or from those in host government agencies.

Here again the evaluator needs to strike a note of realism. The question that he faces is not so much whether there is disagreement concerning project objectives—if he looks far enough, he will always find some. The question is whether the differing interests in the project are fundamentally compatible with the effective accomplishment of certain aims or objectives. Realization of the emphasis and desires of the others by each group is a first step toward compatibility. Later, project participants can take steps to secure a wider sphere of agreement and/or understanding among the several groups or at least to minimize the potential conflict in purposes as project activities are launched.

The initial statement of objectives, aims, and goals may be vague or ill-defined because of lack of time. Some projects are begun rapidly, either because of emergency conditions or because of time factors associated with project approval and financing. It is easy to decry such haste and label it as inappropriate to a university project, but the practicalities of administration and politics will always produce a few instances of this kind. The evaluator needs a different set of glasses to view such undertakings, much as a special set of standards must be applied to the premature baby in its first months and years of life. Operations in the first months of such a project may have to be heavily devoted to working out purposes that can be made operational.

In other cases a clear statement of project objectives may be difficult or even embarrassing, and the evaluator may find that he, too, must be circumspect in what he reports. For example, to go into detail as to how a project is to have a major impact on thousands of members of target groups—such as students of economics at the host country's universities—may raise such a storm of protest that the entire project would have to be cancelled. To suggest that a chemistry teaching project at one university is likely to have an impact on all chemistry professors at that university or all universities may build up tremendous opposition. To suggest that a chemistry demonstration teaching project would have an impact on non-chemistry faculty members because the superior teaching methods introduced would eventually be copied elsewhere, would be unwise. While the spread effect of a project is a very important element, it may not be something that can be candidly identified.

The other side of the coin of public relations is that apparently clearly stated objectives or aims may be set forth for purely formalistic reasons or for public consumption. The list of purposes may thus be both incomplete and overly pretentious at the same time. Erring on the side of including objectives not seriously contemplated is in part a product of the different perspectives of the host country groups, financial sponsors, and the American university. To please the latter two groups, the former may agree to an objective or two that it feels is either unimportant or unwise. The other two parties may engage in similar activity. Thus the formal list of objectives may emphasize direct teaching by the American visiting professors instead of specifying that they will engage in demonstration teaching and "training the trainers." The latter, if spelled out, might raise faculty objections whereas the former merely provides extra professors to share the teaching burdens. The initiators of the project may fully agree that it is the latter two activities that are needed and desired.

The approach to a formal list of objectives, aims, and goals must be one of caution and circumspection whether they are listed in a contract or outlined in a report. They may be a reasonably accurate portrayal of the hopes and expectations of the originators of a project; they may be far from that. In addition, purposes may have been modified in the course of the project.

If at least some consensus as to project objectives is not forth-coming, the project should not go forward. Still, even viable proj-ects will vary in the degree of consensus on purposes and candor in expressing it. A project whose purposes are clearly understood, stated, and agreed upon has a tremendous advantage over one whose purposes are ill defined, or subject to major reservations by one or more of the parties to the undertaking.

Among the serious consequences of unclear objectives is that a project is likely to drift without the steadying influence of a firm rudder of fixed purposes. The criteria for inclusion and ex-clusion of project activities not being evident, the undertaking becomes whatever each individual participant makes it. Parts of the project may work at cross-purposes. One professor may get involved directly with a government agency such as the education ministry and another with a part of a host university such as a school of education. At best, a lack of clarity or candor in the objectives, aims, and goals of a project will result in a general slowdown in project execution while some kind of consensus and operational strategy are devised. Each may develop training programs of a similar kind that are unnecessarily duplicative.

A professor is carrying out a study; to him the project means the completion of his research. A professor is teaching two classes; to him the project means doing the best job possible in the classroom. A professor is advising a government agency; to him the project means being a good consultant. Thus activities are confused with objectives, objectives with intermediate aims, and the latter with broader goals. The activities of the moment become the *raison d'etre*. The host country participants of the moment become the ultimate group for impact. And institution-building is beyond focus.

Without careful consideration of purposes, project adminis-trators may embrace unrealistic or undesirable objectives and aims. The in-service training programs of the ministry of educa-tion or the school of education may concentrate upon training teachers from all over the country. From a superficial point of view this may seem laudable and give the project impressive statistics to report on the number of persons trained. However, it may be far more practical to confine one or both operations to the training of trainers, with regional centers taking on the major burden of training the teachers directly.

An assessment of project purposes from a broad perspective is an essential initial step in the evaluation process.

Multiple Purposes

Throughout this discussion of purposes, I have used the plural rather than the singular. There probably never has been a project that has had a lone objective, aim, or goal. In terms of the ends sought, the simplest university project is probably one that centers around research, and even here the immediate objectives are far greater than the mere completion of a given research assignment. For example, a survey of economic conditions may be undertaken for the value of the research results, for the training of host country nationals in research methods, and as a demonstration of the value an economic research center could have. Multiple objectives, aims, and goals are always present.

Because of their inevitability, decrying the existence of multiple purposes is a meaningless action. Making project participants and their superiors aware of the several purposes is a constructive one. It is frequently true that the rich variety of purposes behind a project is not recognized by the parties most directly involved. Each tends to focus on those aspects of the project that interest him most. The American professor abroad may concentrate on his immediate task of teaching, research, or consultation, and his host country counterparts may do the same. The head of the university group at home may look at the project primarily in terms of what it can do for the university, and a host country director may view it only in terms of his own institution. Even personnel associated with financial sponsors may have special, rather than general, interests relative to a project. "Project generalists" are in short supply.

Awareness of multiple purposes should be accompanied by some set of priorities among them. For example, is research and publication a pressing matter, or can it wait until host country faculty members receive further training? Are the study habits of students something that must be changed at all costs or are the demonstration and introduction of new teaching techniques of paramount importance? What is the relative urgency of modification of courses and curricula compared to the other objectives? An additional question of priority arises where a project covers more than one profession or discipline. If an engineering school is to be strengthened, what stress should be placed upon the basic sciences in the liberal arts faculty?

The several intermediate aims and broad goals also present alternatives that should be ranked in terms of importance. In the early years of a project, many of the university projects—perhaps most—have had to choose between developing a host country staff and organization designed to "train the trainers" (institution-building), and the direct training of some members of target groups. If the former choice is made, relatively few students or trainees pass through the university-assisted program during the first year or two. If the latter, many pass through and receive training, perhaps directly from American professors, since it may take years to recruit and educate an adequate number of local professors. Even such broad goals as assisting host country development, contributing to effective foreign policy, or advancing knowledge require rank ordering if a project is to be effective in the long run.

The different objectives, aims, and goals of a project being often so diverse, selecting one for priority obviously means that others are set aside. Over a given two- or three-year period, there may be little that enriching the American university's program at home has to do with assisting host country development. Foreign policy goals may not be furthered by research projects that advance knowledge. Frequently conflicts arise between institution-building and the training of target groups. And especially if a university project has only a limited number of American professors, as is usually the case, it will not be possible to attain all specific objectives at once.

Partly the matter of conflict among the ends sought is a timing problem, involving the sequence in which they are sought as well as the total time span over which the expected changes are to take place. If a project's life is expected to be two or three years, a maximum of conflict among the many ends is likely. If the life of a project is five or six years, much more accommodation among the several purposes is possible. In addition, the longer time span permits a superior ordering of the sequences of the various objectives, aims, and goals.

For example, it is possible that both institution-building and target-group training aims can be accommodated only if a project's duration is six or more years. Logically, the institution-building aim must precede, and this requires that a few years be allowed for development of host country professors, organization, courses, and curricula. Once the institution is fully under way, it will take some years before the training of trainers (e.g., in-service training directors or instructors in smaller colleges or specialized training institutions) has advanced to the point that they, in turn, are training large numbers of the target groups (e.g., government employees or teachers in elementary and secondary schools).

The conflict among the different ends of a project is not entirely of a sequential or time duration nature. There may be genuine disagreement among the different groups that participate in a project as to its aims or objectives. The compromise on the ends to be sought that usually characterizes the working out of the initial project contract may have reflected only superficial agreement, made possible by failure to attach priorities to the several purposes.

The differences among individuals within groups are also most pronounced when priorities are considered. Latent opposition to overseas involvement at most American universities can be assuaged by including in the list of objectives and goals those activities that will help build up the institution at home. Reluctant faculty members may be brought along to at least a position of neutrality, particularly if it can be demonstrated that research and teaching at home will be furthered by embracing the project. It usually happens, however, that project activities that would be most supportive of such perspectives are among those that are not present in the first year or two of a project. This may pose a problem for project managers who seek the cooperation of many faculty members.

Unstated Purposes

Like multiple aims and objectives, unstated purposes are almost always present in university projects abroad. Also unstated are the diverse motivations that lie behind them. Unstated project ends may be just as meritorious, just as laudable, as those in the formal contract list. The contract list may be too brief or the contract may be an inappropriate place to specify some of the project objectives. Whatever the reason for their being unstated, it can be assumed that every major participating group and every major program participant has some objectives, aims, and goals that are not in the formal list.

If the project managers and program participants are to carry out the project in a sophisticated manner, they should begin by trying to become aware of the unstated objectives of other individuals and groups. Only by so doing can they be sensitive to the mosaic of purposes of which the project is composed. Unless the project is seen from the point of view of each of the major individual and group participants, those responsible for evaluation will end up with unrealistic results. This is not to say that project evaluators should set forth clearly in writing that which has been unwritten but understood. But the written evaluation and the informal comments of the evaluation team should take cognizance of the total environment of the project, including the unstated objectives and aims.

If the evaluators of a project abroad are to come to know and appreciate its unstated as well as its formal purposes, additional time in the field must be taken. An appreciation of the significance of unstated objectives comes principally through familiarity with the groups and individuals concerned.

There is nothing unique about university projects abroad with respect to unstated purposes. Unstated purposes underlie most group activity everywhere. Consultants to an American university strive to identify unstated purposes before they proceed to substantive recommendations. Such a procedure is part and parcel of getting to know the "inside" of an organization or undertaking.

What are some of the unstated purposes of a project? A number of them center around the hopes and fears of the principal participants, their desire to be professionally and personally successful and to be perceived by others as such. In less developed countries, positions are often prized more for the status they bring than for the program leadership opportunities they present. A dean of a school of engineering in a host country may be looked upon by American professors as occupying a role of innovation and leadership in engineering. The dean and his colleagues may look upon his position as bringing significant prestige to him and his family, including title, remuneration, and certain prerogatives. They may have embraced the project principally to reinforce status variables of this kind or, alternatively, to attain such variables while at the same time subscribing to formal project purposes not in conflict with them. Each major participant, American or host country national, has his own reasons for participating in the project. These reasons become project objectives or objectives associated with the project for the person concerned.

There are unstated group objectives of a status or prestige nature that parallel those of the individual participants. An American university may undertake an overseas assignment for several reasons, some of which will not be found in formal project documents. A university has a number of roles, and they intersect at numerous points. A project must be considered in relation to a university's status and prestige, its major clientele, its support base, and its continuing contacts with the project's financial sponsors and host country groups. A project may bring a measure of institutional prestige, particularly if similar universities also have such projects. It may further the university's relations with the financial sponsor in other programs. A project may extend intimate working relations already existing between the American and host country institution, or it may cement personal friendships such as between the principal officers of the two universities.

One of the most common unstated objectives is a desire for the material advantages a project may bring. A host country university, without adequate laboratories for science instruction and research, may value a project primarily for the physical equipment it hopes to receive. In the early days of university contracting, there were several instances of equipment being desired for prestige, rather than the use to which it could be put. Expensive scientific machines were displayed outside dean's offices but not made operational, a practice incomprehensible to the visiting American faculty members but understandable in terms of local cultural values. Such incidents have been rare, but it has been common for a host university to value the equipment a project brings more than the advice of the visiting professors.

Some American universities have sought contracts for financial advantage. The costs of carrying out a project abroad are however such that this is not a sound objective in the long run. Most projects barely pay their own way and some undoubtedly cost the American university money if all project-related activities are considered. But the American university may indirectly receive a material return from overseas contracts. Being active in projects abroad may place the university in a better position to seek foundation grants and government research contracts in the international area.

Participants may join a project in part for the material rewards that are present. A contract-assisted portion of a host university may be able to offer higher salaries and better working conditions. Air-conditioned offices and automobiles, extra pay for research projects, and trips overseas may be among the attractions. The American professor may be similarly motivated by the opportunity to take his family abroad for a year or two. Such motivations may not substantially affect the formal project objectives if strong professional reasons for participating are also present. In their absence, personal participation may be like the expensive piece of equipment outside the dean's office: showy, but operationally ineffective.

Overseas, the objectives, aims, and goals of a project may be either stated or unstated because of the effects they have on intergroup or interpersonal relations. Projects have an impact on intergroup and interpersonal relations in many ways. Reference has already been made to situations in which to specify all the purposes of a project would be to insure maximum opposition to it, especially among those indirectly affected. There may be competition among the schools and colleges of a university, and a technical assistance project may be a means of one school moving ahead more rapidly. There may be a disagreement among the deans and faculty members as to pro- and anti-American attitudes, and a pro-American dean may move ahead to embrace a project. If there is enough anti-American feeling in other quarters, the project may have rough sledding.

At an American university, a new project abroad may stamp a particular college as an especially active one and move it ahead in the eyes of the president of the university. At the same time, the project may give a college or school an image of ignoring problems at home and placing a higher priority on overseas operations than on teaching and research. Since there is normally some latent opposition in the faculty to such enterprises, the role of the college or school at home must be carefully considered before going ahead with a contract abroad.

A project may be largely the product of a single staff member's interest. The university's approval of the undertaking, whether it be a host country or American institution, may be formal, and not a matter of deep conviction of the institution as a whole. Thus the purposes of a project may become intertwined with the personal objectives of the project entrepreneur.

The participants may find relations with their colleagues altered as a result of project involvement. Sometimes these relations may be affected favorably, sometimes unfavorably. An American university professor may feel forgotten by his colleagues at home, and be fearful of his professional future. A host country national may find that the doctorate that he has acquired has given him new respect from his associates. Whether the results are favorable or unfavorable, changes in interpersonal relations brought about by projects may become more important than substantive objectives.

Project purposes may be unstated because of the reluctance of project initiators to state boldly and frankly their future hopes. The desire of a host country dean to have his school of business administration serve as a major graduate institution for students from a large region embracing several countries may best be kept hidden when the school has not yet held its first course.

American universities seldom set forth in formal project documents exactly what contribution to long-range institutional goals a particular project may make. A financial sponsor may see a project as a worthwhile experiment or a kind of "foot-in-the-door;" it may not wish to reveal its future strategy. The project evaluator needs to take into account such long-range hopes as well as the stated objectives, aims, and goals.

Adaptation of Purposes

Project purposes always evolve over the course of an undertaking. No matter how carefully the contract is drawn and no matter how excellent the background reports and papers, those who seek to evaluate a project after a year or two or more will not find that the documentation adequately defines project purposes. There are many reasons why this is so, but the major one is that in almost every project, a central responsibility of the project is to clarify the objectives and aims, to give them specific meaning and operational relevance, and to adapt them to the circumstances or environment in which the project finds itself. Even with the maximum of good will, information, and agreement in principle, the project initiators would indeed be foolhardy to specify in great detail and in rather rigid form the objectives, aims, and goals of the undertaking. Each project must adapt itself to its own ecology. Part of the test of its success is the degree to which it has done so effectively.

However detailed the advance planning, some of the specific objectives will remain to be spelled out as project operations move forward. The agreement may call for courses in public health. What kind of courses? What kind of approach? With what interrelations with which administrative agencies of the government? With what recruitment base for students? With what professional future for graduates? Most project agreements have not covered a majority of such points, and yet they are central to both specific objectives and intermediate aims, and not irrelevant to broad goals. Project participants should have a sense of mission that helps them project meaningful courses of action.

The operations of each project bring to light new information, and this in turn requires some adaptation of project purposes. Even in those university projects abroad that have been preceded by a pre-contract team survey of conditions, only a fraction of the information that may be relevant can possibly be assembled and analyzed given the short duration, usually a few months, of the study. The project team that begins the assignment is more numerous than the survey group and its stay is far longer. A similar commitment of personnel and time occurs on the host country side. Soon both the level of information about the project and the ecological factors that impinge on it are immeasurably raised. Project objectives and aims must be adjusted accordingly.

Furthermore, as the months turn into years, the ecology of the project changes due to factors over which it has no control whatsoever. Policy changes within the Agency for International Development may have a major effect on the project. These may be Washington- or field-induced. For example, the Washington policies of broader cooperation with American universities which began under the leadership of former administrator David Bell have affected most university projects overseas. A change in field personnel—perhaps a new mission director—can quite completely alter the balance of forces that determines project purposes. Within the host country major political shifts occur, and these can result in fuller cooperation or more resistance to project operations. Each undertaking exists in an environment that is changing constantly. Project administrators must be sensitive to these changes and adapt their purposes accordingly.

The project itself hopefully brings about changes, some anticipated and others not. Project purposes may be affected by these induced changes. A simple case is illustrative. A project is unusually successful and develops a new agriculture curriculum a year earlier than planned. Additional objectives then become possible. Larger numbers of students can pass through the courses. Field research can be undertaken where it was out of the question before. If, on the other hand, the progress of a project is unduly slow, its purposes must be scaled down to more realistic levels.

The evaluation process itself is inevitably a part of the progressive identification of purposes. One of the salutary effects of annual or biennial evaluation is to help clarify the aims and objectives of a project and to sharpen, confirm, or modify them as appropriate. Therefore, the evaluation process is not one in which a complete statement of purposes is obtained in advance and project accomplishments set against them. Rather, the adequacy of the original formulations of purposes is judged in the light of changing circumstances, and the project's modifications of them considered in relation to the problems it has faced and the opportunities it has encountered.

Benchmarks and Measurement

The evaluation of university projects overseas that begins with an assessment of project purposes loses much of its meaning unless the conditions that existed when the project was initiated are clearly identified. Equally important is the identification of current conditions against which future objectives and aims can be projected. Thus there are two parallel but quite different functions to be performed in project evaluation: first, an historical assessment of original project purposes and how they related to the conditions that existed; and, second, a current assessment of project purposes and how they relate to conditions that now exist. For projects of long duration, there is a possibility of a series of intermediate assessments, so that the adaptation of project purposes can successively be placed against the changes in the conditions that exist.

Initial Benchmarks

Most university projects abroad suffer from project administrators not knowing precisely the point from which the projects began. Adequate benchmarks—detailed descriptions and measurements, environmental factors that affect projects or that the projects are expected to alter, which must be collected before the projects begin—are among the most difficult project data to come by.

Superficially, adequate benchmarks would seem easy to collect. If the technical assistance program calls for a new school of medicine, a survey team is dispatched to the country and stays there until it collects the data that are needed—enrollment at any existing medical schools; incidence of disease; proportion of physicians to population and desired or needed proportion to handle the medical problem; the gap between what exists and what is needed; the kind of medical schools that exist including character of students, faculty, and curricula and the kind that is needed; the amount of money and personnel put into the existing system and the amount of money and personnel needed for the proposed system. The list could be expanded, contracted, or refined by *a priori* reasoning as the situation warrants, so that a logical and complete set of data would seem assured. Then why the difficulty? Why do rational, capable university personnel not see the need for adequate benchmark data and meet that need?

After fifteen years of university contracting abroad, one fact is evident: the survey parties from most universities have been new at the process of foreign technical assistance in a good share of the instances. Consequently, they have not realized the importance of obtaining substantial data for benchmarks. They have concentrated on the immediate task at hand: recommending or failing to recommend involvement for their institution and specifying some of the conditions appropriate to such involvement. Project operation and evaluation have not been uppermost in their minds. They have not begun with an *a priori* list of items of data that would be logically desirable and even necessary to collect.

Second, the circumstances under which initial surveys have been carried out have not been conducive to securing adequate benchmark data. Survey parties have often been organized hurriedly, with at most a month or two for preparation. The members of the survey team have spent most of this time finishing up many of their regular responsibilities so that they can get away with a "clean desk." There has been almost no time to do advance planning or research. Briefing has been minimal. Upon arrival abroad, the survey team has found itself in an environment where immediate issues of policy concerning a proposed new school, college, or institute have dominated their attention.

Team members seldom number more than two or three, and they seldom stay more than a month or two. The result is some rather quick impressions, but strikingly inadequate benchmark data. If team members were released from their regular jobs for a month or two before going abroad to undertake preliminary planning and then were allowed (or required) to put in a longer number of man-months abroad—perhaps doubling the typical number—far better results would accrue.

Even with great experience and adequate time, survey teams have difficulty getting adequate benchmark data, because relevant data often do not exist, at least in readily available form. A medical school survey team probably finds rough data on most of the topics in which it is interested, but there are inadequacies and actual gaps. Incidence of disease and number of physicians are examples of data that can normally be obtained in an approximate form. Total enrollment at existing medical schools can also be ascertained. However, many of the data taken for granted at American universities are not available for host country institutions. Background of students, grades, dropout rate, library holdings, library usage—these and countless other items of information are frequently not available. Information on secondary schools—particularly on the adequacy of secondary education and the nature of entry into secondary schools—is often lacking. Budget and personnel data are usually hard to obtain, at least in terms meaningful for educational planning; it is sometimes impossible to determine full-time staff equivalents, let alone full-time student equivalents. Information that would relate the medical school effort to broader socio-economic planning may be entirely lacking. Data that are available are often not in usable form, and data processing is far from automatic, making cross-classifications impossible.

Some data that are needed are essentially obtainable only through informal means. The actual content of a course that a host country professor has been teaching and the nature of his relations with the students can only be ascertained by gaining the confidence of professor and students or those immediately associated with them. Resistances to change in the host university are also difficult to identify, except after a long period of personal acquaintance with the institutional environment. Data of this character can more readily be collected by those stationed in the country for some years, such as representatives of the financial sponsor, be it a foundation or AID. Unfortunately, sponsor's representatives have only infrequently undertaken such an assignment systematically, in advance of a survey team.

Even under ideal circumstances, a survey team is not going to be able to anticipate all the useful benchmark data for a project. Key factors concerning the project will evolve and change along with the project itself. It is the responsibility of project administrators to obtain data on such factors as they are identified from time to time. In addition, for those projects for which inadequate benchmarks were set forth by the survey team, project participants would do well to rectify the shortcoming at the beginning of the project.

Project evaluators also have their responsibilities for identifying an adequate set of benchmarks and obtaining the necessary data. In interim evaluations—those that take place during the course of a project—evaluation teams can play major roles in relating project purposes to benchmark data and collecting, or requesting that project participants collect, the necessary data. In this manner, adequate benchmarks will be available for the duration of the project, and will be important not only in the final evaluation, but for the continual assessment of progress and the adjustment of objectives with evidence of progress, that characterizes any well-run project.

Identifying and measuring or otherwise describing benchmarks is a continual process for which project sponsor, survey team, project administrator, and evaluator share responsibility. Benchmarks should be obtained as early in the life of a project as possible, but a completely satisfactory set is likely to be highly elusive, even in the best planned and executed overseas contracts.

Measuring Change

Since a majority of university projects abroad involve higher education, there are many areas in which quantifiable data would be possible. In our own society higher education has become highly quantified and subject to computer-analyzed data. While faculty skeptics demur, institutional research specialists, admission officers, and registrars have pushed far ahead in measuring higher education, including its quality-associated characteristics. With this extensive American experience behind them, why cannot American universities simply take the statistical techniques, say of the Big Ten and Chicago group of universities, and apply them abroad to provide an effective and comparable measure of institutional progress and educational achievement?

As a long-range objective, such a standardized concept may have some merit, but it does not have much applicability to pre-project planning or initial project operations. As has already been pointed out, many of the data are not readily available in the host countries, and trained university statisticians are not to be found. It would take several years of intensive technical assistance to develop educational measurement to a substantial degree of sophistication. A number of universities have assisted host country institutions in this area, and improvement has normally been marked. But such a process does not provide reliable initial benchmarks for project use.

Strong objections will often be found on the part of host country students or faculty to quantifying some aspects of higher education. Data on student achievement obtained through examination imply changes that seems near-revolutionary to host country participants. In most situations, course examinations and grades comparable to the American system cannot be introduced even after some years of effort. Achievement or intelligence tests are either not available or not culturally relevant. If they could be developed, they would be unacceptable to students or faculty, although a well-conceived plan for obtaining consent and cooperation might reduce the objections.

There are also large and important areas of project-related concerns that are not readily subject to quantification. There is no ready agreement in the United States as to how the quality of teaching is to be measured, for example. And quite apart from educational measurements, such variables as the degree of resistance to change are important benchmarks for every technical assistance endeavor.

With full acknowledgment of these and other difficulties, project administrators should explore more widely the possibilities of some uniform approach to measuring benchmarks and change. University projects are numerous and apparently are to continue for some time to come. They could be made more effective by more systematic identification of key project variables and more effective measurement of change. Two steps could be taken rather readily. First, since there have been many serious efforts at the evaluation of projects, the research instruments of these studies could be taken as representative of the benchmark and progress data that are needed. A manual of suggestions compiled from such sources would be exceedingly useful. Second, the techniques of institutional research in the United States could be reviewed, and items identified that would be most useful overseas. Again, a loose-leaf collection of such devices or techniques would be helpful. The American Council on Education should consider sponsoring such efforts.

Causes and Results

Evaluation readily implies objectives or goals, benchmarks or starting points, progress or change, and some way of measuring or describing them. The process of evaluation is interlaced with many conceptual difficulties as well, and the evaluator is constantly faced with making value judgments, rather than being a mere reporter of the "facts" of the case.

Terminological Distinctions

Project evaluation requires a sharp distinction between *changes* that have taken place and *results* that have accrued from project operations. The former is rather readily determined providing that adequate benchmarks are available. The latter is exceedingly difficult to determine, for it requires a judgment as to the causes of the changes that have been observed. Some university projects abroad find themselves in an environment of change, where the

forces for a better life, broad development, and educational experiment are strong and omnipresent. Changes in the university
system are almost bound to occur under such circumstances, and
the main task of the advisers from the United States may be guid-
ing the lines of change, not trying to induce it. Some desired
changes might have occurred even if no technical assistance effort
had been launched.

The isolation of the independent variables (project operations)
is not especially difficult. Nor is the identification of the dependent
variables (project objectives, aims, and goals) troublesome. The
problem occurs with the numerous and almost uncontrollable
intervening variables. No technical assistance project exists in
isolation. It is part of the large social fabric of the host country.
The forces that play upon it are numerous. Two similar projects
which follow identical methods of operations to develop new
schools of engineering in countries that are equally advanced in
science education may have entirely different results because of
intervening variables, factors outside the project that are associated with the sought-for changes. There are innumerable possi
ble intervening variables such as the education policies of the
host government, rate of industrialization, degree of national
identity, and foreign policy of the United States.

A distinction also needs to be made between the *means* and
ends of project operations. The progression of specific objectives,
intermediate aims, and broad goals suggests that there is an
interconnected chain of means and ends from the most specific
project activity to the broadest goal. In project evaluation, it is
imperative to keep two things in mind. First, progress in project
activity is not the same as progress in meeting objectives, and,
likewise, progress in meeting objectives is not the same thing as
achieving aims or goals. For example, American professors may
teach many courses in the host institution but there is no guarantee
that this will result in introducing new teaching techniques in
courses handled by host country professors. In turn, new teaching techniques may be introduced but no institution-building or
educating of key target groups take place. Sometimes projects
are successful at the level of project activity, but not at the level

of objectives, and success in achieving objectives does not necessarily bring success in terms of intermediate aims and broad
goals. Second, there are values attached to each mean and each
end, and the support base for each project is determined in large
part by the balance that is achieved among them by project administrators. It should never be assumed that the broader goals
are valued more intensively than the specific objectives. Quite the
reverse is often the case. One of the tasks of evaluation is to review the values attached to different project activities, objectives,
aims, and goals and determine whether project personnel have
used a set of means and attained a set of ends that promise adequate support and an effective role for the changed institution.

Both *accommodative* and *substantive change* occur in every
project. The former should help give rise to desired substantive
change, but this simple relationship does not entirely represent
the case in most projects. Accommodative change is change resulting from the very fact that a project exists, apart from the
content of a project. It is administrative or managerial in character. On both the host country and American sides, responsibilities
of certain officials may be altered, salaries and other costs
modified, organizational arrangements adjusted, and office space
assigned. If a project is to have desired substantive content, there
must be adequate supportive accommodative change. Suitable administrative methods must be selected, and appropriate personnel
policies pursued. On the other hand, it is possible for a project to
expend much of its energies on such accommodative items, and
ignore or downgrade the real purposes of the project.

Substantive change relates to the content of a project, but is
more inclusive than objectives, aims, and goals. Substantive
change includes the latter but may also include undesired changes
in content. There are often negative as well as positive consequences flowing from an undertaking. To commit resources in one
direction means not committing them to another. To develop a
curriculum with one approach means de-emphasizing or ignoring
another. And the curriculum that is chosen may assist one aspect
of economic development and hurt another.

The Nature of Change

University projects abroad exist primarily for the purpose of introducing changes in the host country. They do so in three principle ways: *transmitting* culture items from the United States to the host country, with minor or major adaptations; *creating* or helping to create new culture items in the host country; and *reviving* or *rediscovering* appropriate local cultural values. The impact of a project may appear to be greater, at least in the short run, if it is emphasizing transmitted culture items without major adaptations and much less if it is concerned principally with creation of new culture items or reviving traditional values in modified form. To develop a new breed of cattle for host country conditions (creating a new culture item) will take infinitely longer than shipping cattle from the United States for upgrading herds (transmitting a culture item). To develop new textbooks will take longer than translating those in use elsewhere. The creation of new culture items or the reviving of local cultural values is not necessarily preferable to the transmission of existing ones; indeed, the three usually are found side by side in the same project. The mixture of the three and their appropriateness are among the focal points of project evaluation. Comparisons among projects may be highly misleading if the relative degree of transmitting, creating, and reviving is not kept in mind.

Innovations vary in their *number* and in their *weights*. In initial conception, some projects call for many changes and others for few. To create a new university in a country that has had none before requires innovation every step of the way. To carry out research on a disease that is a major public health problem may require few innovations. Because one project results in many more innovations than another does not mean that it is any more successful even if equal time and money has been put in both. The difference may inhere in the character of the projects.

One change may be infinitely more fundamental or radical than another. To assist the Philippines in higher education has been easier than assisting universities in many other countries because of the greater similarity in institutional practices with the United States. A new form of examination may not be a matter of great concern to a country that has not had a long history of higher education. It may be a matter of great principle to a country like India where expectations of students, professors, employers, and parents are all based on the current system.

University projects abroad are faced with *time* dimensions of their undertakings. Formally, a project will be planned for a certain number of years during which it is hoped that certain changes can be introduced. However, it is unrealistic to assume that a project which is to last four years will, if all goes well, acomplish a quarter of the planned innovations every twelve months. Change is commonly erratic. The literature is filled with references to points of "breakthrough." Consequently, an interim evaluation faces a difficult problem of judgment in determining whether satisfactory progress has been made.

There is no unilinear pattern to innovation. It is true that many projects begin slowly and then accelerate the pace of innovation in the latter years of the project. But in some cases, the situation is the reverse. Certainly in regard to immediate project activities, the major changes are likely to take place with the initiation of the project. If a new college of engineering is being established, most of the courses and curricula, all new, will be established before it opens its doors, although it may take a long time before the host country professors can handle such courses, with due regard for approach, content, and quality.

In a broad sense, every project activity results in change in the same manner that action brings forth reaction. It may not bring forth change in the desired person or group and it may not be the kind of change that is sought, but change will occur. Often there is a certain amount of trial and error. It is not easy to bring about the innovations that American universities are called upon to assist in their projects abroad. There are no sure formulae. Consequently, one characteristic that distinguishes a good project is its sensitivity to the impact or lack that its operations are having. The American project participants must be as receptive as anyone to adaptation and change from project "feedback."

Change begets change. This obvious statement has important consequences for university overseas activities. In the evaluation of the accomplishment of a project, the progress that has been made in regard to successive waves of impact should be assessed. If target institutions or individuals are not those immediately involved in a project, a series of intermediaries must be influenced or affected first before the hoped-for result can be attained. The training of instructors of teacher training institutions may take some years. Ultimately, the curricula of these institutions may change and then the teachers who receive training at them will feel an impact. Finally, the students in the classroom will receive improved education and be able to contribute to the development of their country more effectively. Project accomplishment should be analyzed in terms of the succeeding waves of impact that it has had. However, waves become progressively smaller and less distinguishable as they become farther removed from the stone that was dropped in the water. Similarly, impact of university projects becomes only one of many factors that influence the course of events for far-removed target institutions or persons, and sometimes not a very significant one.

The wave effect is also evident within the institution or group of host country participants most immediately associated with the project. The introduction of a new curriculum may require a substantial increase in acquisitions for the library, and these, in turn, may necessitate a larger and more highly skilled library staff. Also, a new curriculum may require some additions to the faculty, and perhaps further training for those already on the faculty. New secretarial help may be called for. New recruiting methods and admission standards for students, and perhaps a new student clientele may follow. The impact of a single change may substantially affect an entire institution.

Inter-Project Comparisons

As university technical assistance programs have expanded in number, comparisons among them have inevitably been made. University A's "successful" program is contrasted with university B's "unsuccessful" undertaking. Officials of the Ford Foundation, the Agency for International Development, or a similar financial sponsor and host country nationals make comparisons between university and non-university projects, such as those administered directly by the financial sponsor and those undertaken by private contractors. Of course, to some extent the evaluation of one project is based upon a judgment as to the success that other projects have, or might have, had.

University Project Comparisons

The casual commentator on university projects abroad often makes sweeping comparisons of projects of one type or in one field or in one geographical area with those in quite another. While eschewing such all-encompassing comparisons, university administrators and professors have made more limited comparisons within countries or subject-matter fields or by types of projects. Such comparisons have been both useful and essential for a constructive approach to evaluation and good project administration. However, even in making more limited comparisons, serious difficulties arise.

First, the kind and amount of change that is sought varies widely among apparently similar projects. Projects are commonly grouped according to subject matter. There are so many public administration, so many teacher training, so many engineering, and so many health and medical projects. Even within each group, no two projects have identical objectives. Public administration projects may appear to have a kind of similarity of outlook and purpose. However, one project may be aimed at developing a graduate school of public administration at the main national university (University of Michigan, Philippines), another at developing a non-degree post-graduate training institution (Syracuse University, Pakistan), a third at developing in-service training (Indiana University, Indonesia), and a fourth at consultation and advice to government agencies (a portion of Michigan State University, Viet Nam). Inter-project comparisons become exceedingly difficult under such circumstances.

To extend the problems of comparison further, universities working to strengthen graduate instruction in public administration do so under a wide variety of circumstances. In one case they may be strengthening a program already underway. In another, a new program may have been decided upon. In still another, the hope may be that support for a permanent program may eventually be forthcoming by having an American university team invited to the host institution.

Second, the resistances to change that are confronted by apparently similar projects vary widely. Resistances vary by both degree and type. Some American universities have entered upon projects where few host country personnel have wanted the project (University of California, Italy; University of Tennessee, Bolivia). In other cases, similar projects have been welcomed, if not by an entire university, at least by those principally concerned (University of Michigan, University of the Philippines; University of Minnesota, Seoul National University). If the latter condition prevails, a close cooperation between the American university and host country personnel may be relatively easy to establish. While such close cooperation can stem from a pre-university contract group of host country professors who are pleased with the project, it is more frequent that it comes from a staff of new professors who have undergone special training as a result of project operations and who are therefore dedicated to major project purposes.

If major opposition to a project exists, its first few years may have to be devoted to eliciting the cooperation, understanding, and dedication of host country participants to project objectives. In terms of evaluation, such a project must be considered several years behind a seemingly similar one that finds ready enthusiasm for the undertaking among host country nationals.

The type of resistance to change may also vary from project to project. Each institution must develop its external support base, and this is especially important for one that is undergoing major change. Regardless of whether or not there is a high degree of support among the immediate project participants from the host country, there may be strong or weak support among the institution's more influential friends. These include clientele groups, host government and other financial or legal sponsors, political interests, and business, professional, and other leadership groups.

Even in the same country, two projects may encounter entirely different resistances to change. One may be considered in the mainstream, and have many influential friends as well as a group of devoted professors. Another may be considered unimportant, and it may lack both a general local support and the interest and dedication at the host university.

Third, the general ecological factors that impinge upon a university project abroad—the educational structure, the political system, and economic conditions—are nowhere the same and account for many of the differences in impact from project to project. Great contrasts in educational systems are to be found regionally; for example, in most of the sub-Saharan African countries as compared to South Asia. In the former, university projects encounter exceedingly high rates of illiteracy and a shallow layer of educated elite. With only a handful of university graduates, poor elementary as well as secondary schooling, and no established tradition of higher education, these countries are among the least developed educationally. In South Asia, illiteracy is still high, but there are many universities with distinguished histories, and in urban areas elementary and secondary education is well advanced. The educated elite is so large that unemployment and underemployment exist in serious proportions.

Educational systems vary as to type as well as to extent of their development. Colonial heritages remain very important. Some countries lean heavily in the English direction, others in the French, Belgian, or Dutch. An American university team must adapt its cultural bias to the different conditions it finds in each country. It must seek to understand educational patterns and prejudices of the former colonizer as well as the local culture of the new nation.

The political and administrative systems of the host country can assist or block the progress of a university technical assistance project overseas. There is a wide range of such systems, forcing similar projects to adapt themselves to quite different conditions. The traditionalist leaders of Iran, the military of Korea, the dominant party of India and of Mexico, the competing interest groups and parties of the Philippines—each presents its own special opportunities for impact, each presents its own special clusters of resistances to change. And the same is true of the administrative system—developed or undeveloped as it may be and as influenced by colonial heritage and other factors.

While almost all the countries that have had technical assistance contracts can be roughly classified as less developed economically, there are actually many important economic differences among them that affect university projects. The per capita annual income variations are marked, from less than fifty dollars to several hundred dollars. The crops that account for most of the agricultural production and the pattern and extent of industrialization present vivid contrasts, country to country and province to province. In some instances, the economy is rapidly changing; in others it is stagnant. Overall economic planning may be worked out and enforced in detail in one country; it may be mere window-dressing in another.

Thus one university project may be closely tied in with integrated plans for economic development; the kind of training and the number of trainees to be graduated may be rather rigidly specified, with jobs assured to all graduates. In an apparently similar project in another country, a university project may have little relation to overall planning, and its graduates may have no more than hunting licenses. Similar differences could be described at length.

The differences encountered by university projects are such as to throw caution on any quick comparisons. An evaluation team for a single project is handicapped in placing the experience of the university in perspective unless its members represent experience with other projects. In the future, better comparative data will be available if evaluators accept responsibility for identifying as clearly as possible project purposes, resistances to change, and the general ecological factors that are closely related to project operations and impact.

Alternatives to University Projects

Evaluation of a university project involves an assessment of its costs as well as its impact. Costs are relative. If university personnel are assigned to technical assistance work abroad, they are not directly contributing to teaching or research at home. Thus a balancing of the plus and minus factors affecting university overseas undertakings includes consideration of the alternative uses to which university resources can be put, and the alternative means for carrying out technical assistance abroad.

Of the several alternative means to university technical assistance projects, two are by far the most common—direct administration of the project by the financial sponsor such as a foundation or AID, and contract with a consulting firm. The former has frequently worked well, and as a practical matter, the financial sponsor always is faced with a decision as to whether to do the job directly itself or to contract with an outside group. AID teams in education, economics, agriculture, and public health have carried out projects very similar to those that American universities have undertaken. A decision on which method of project implementation to follow is often based upon administrative considerations—does the sponsoring agency have the capacity to recruit the team at this time; will a university group be too free-wheeling; do the members of the field mission of the sponsoring agency have strong personal preferences?

If the financial sponsor decides not to carry on a project directly, it may choose a consulting firm rather than a university as the vehicle. Consulting firms are accustomed to hiring special personnel for assignments in a variety of locations. A number of them have accumulated considerable overseas experience. They may also be somewhat more amenable to supervision by the financial sponsor in the field, although experience to date is not entirely clear on this matter.

There are still other alternatives to universities. Certain professional associations have taken on project responsibilities. California became the first state to do so. Professional associations and state governments (and even localities) could become more frequent contractors for technical assistance projects abroad. Conceivably, they could carry out projects that would parallel those that have been assigned to universities in the past. The Fulbright program is also being used as an alternative to university projects with university professors selected in nationwide competition after determination of needs by the United States Educational Foundations overseas.

All the alternatives to university projects abroad from time to time make use of university professors, particularly in projects where advanced skills in higher education or in the several disciplines or professions are required. There are three major differences in those cases where universities are not the contractors: personnel are recruited on a national basis rather than in large part from a single institution, university professors are a somewhat smaller proportion of total project professional personnel, and a university does not have institutional responsibility for the project.

A complete evaluation of university projects must therefore consider not just the potential effectiveness of alternative forms of technical assistance but also the distinctive characteristics of university projects. It is in their institution-related aspects that the latter are different. This may be partly reflected in the heavy proportion of professors and staff members from the home institution that serve abroad. It may be found in the institutional responsibility for project success. It may be evident in the investment of institutional prestige behind the project, the possibility of a continuing university-to-university association, or at least a continuing American university interest in the country concerned as the result of "feedback" to the home campus of project-created interests.

Institution-related values are maximized in projects that associate university with university, but may be present to some degree in undertakings that bring a university in close contact with a training institute or a government agency such as a department of education. The key is not the kind of host country organization with which a university is associated. Rather, it is the desire of the American university to allocate institutional resources to the project because of the continuing institutional values that are thereby achieved. What is appropriate for a university to undertake is dependent on how it has defined its mission and allocated its resources. If international programs are not an integral part of the development plan of an American university, it should not get involved in them.

Field evaluation is thus intimately bound up with home institution evaluation. To be appropriate for a university, a project must effectively relate itself to home objectives and purposes. Close connections between field staff and home institution should obtain. If these conditions are not present, the appropriateness of a university undertaking the assignment may be severely questioned. Direct hire or a consulting firm may be a preferable alternative.

Methods of Evaluation

Evaluation of university projects abroad should be a continuing process and closely related to program planning and administration. There is a place for a terminal evaluation, to sum up the progress that was made during the course of a completed project. Such an evaluation can be helpful in determining future program commitments and strategies on the part of the host government, financial sponsor, and American university, and it can also provide a useful base of comparison for other projects. But for maximum usefulness, evaluation should take place during the course of a project so that its operations can be adjusted to project conditions and prospects as effectively as possible.

Internal and External Evaluations

In a sense, each project participant engages in continuous assessment of impact as he adjusts his own activities to the changes taking place in his environment. Perceptive participants, with sensitive antenna that receive messages from the several sources centrally concerned with the project, can be quite effective in this informal process. Formal short-term evaluation, organized by project administrators, is nonetheless essential in a project of any substantial size.

Evaluation can be built into project administration in several ways. A well-organized system of weekly staff meetings can concentrate selectively on certain aspects of the operations to assess problems and impact. Periodic staff reports are a second method. Library statistics, enrollment statistics, and grade analyses are among the numerical data that may be appropriate. Surveys of clientele groups and alumni, reviews of curriculum development, and assessment of teaching methods are examples of studies that may add additional depth to project evaluation.

A more extensive method of evaluation involves a review of a project annually or biennially by the parties concerned either individually or collectively. It is perhaps this phase of evaluation that has fallen shortest of being effective. A university dean, vice-president, or president may make a trip abroad and stay a week or so. He talks with project personnel, host country officials, and the field mission of the financial sponsor. He makes a brief report, sometimes in writing, and moves quickly on, for his time is at a premium. A few universities have combined this procedure with a preliminary report prepared by project participants, so that the visiting dignitary can have a quick orientation to project problems and progress, preferably short enough so that it can be carried along and read in the airplane during the course of the trip.

It is easy to make a parody of such evaluations. However, they are essential to project operations, even though they may not play a key role in evaluation. The dean, vice-president, and president must understand a project if institutional resources are to be effectively committed, and if institutional feedback is to be maximized. These university officials are symbols of university commitment to a project, and a visit, however short, has a salutary effect. While they seldom stay long enough to make a definitive evaluation, because of their position they may be able to find out information that eludes project administrators. Particularly in relations with high-level officials of the host institution and government and the financial sponsor, their position and rank may bring them access not available to others. They have a breadth of experience that permits them to see the larger picture. They speak authoritatively, thus settling certain issues that may otherwise remain the subject of debate.

Rather than decry such visits, it is better to place them in a total plan for project evaluation. Intensive annual program review sessions that last a week or two and involve project officials of each of the three groups (university, host, and sponsor) can be a useful first step. These can be made more effective through careful advanced analysis of project purposes and impact to date by staff members. The merit of all three groups participating is that evaluation can be integrated into project operations more thoroughly if all parties examine purposes and progress together. If they undertake separate evaluations, their perspectives may vary, and close cooperation be made more difficult. Working closely together in an evaluation exercise is a uniting process; if the opportunity exists, it should not be passed by. A visit by a university president after such a process has been completed may be highly valuable.

If proper internal evaluations are made, outside assessment is useful or necessary only on occasion—perhaps every three or four years. Broad studies of universities and their roles abroad help shape national policy and influence the course of university involvement. A concentrated study of the experience of a single project may provide vivid detail as to the policies and methods that can effectively be pursued under a given set of conditions. In addition, an outside evaluation can lend an assurance of objectivity which often eludes those carried out internally. Where there is division among the major parties of a project, an outside judgment may prove useful. The prestige of a recognized outside observer may also be of advantage to the project by bringing welcome recognition. On occasion leaders of a project may want an outside observer in a field of specialization or with an experience not represented on the team itself. The new insights forthcoming may lead to new opportunities. An assessment by someone outside the project may at first appear to be a saving of staff time, but there is little gained in this respect, since staff members must spend considerable blocks of time with any such person. To ease the difficulty of obtaining able outside assessment, the American Council on Education or Education and World Affairs could offer services in assembling evaluation teams.

Problems

Whether the evaluation be carried out by a team or by a single person, it is often faced with many problems. At the very least, the evaluator needs to be sensitive to their potential presence. In some ways, evaluation problems are similar to those encountered in identifying project objectives at the contract-writing stage.

There may be time pressure. The university president who spends only a week abroad may do so because his schedule does not permit more time. However, frequently project personnel feel equally pressed and are happy to have him leave after only a week. They want to get back to the practical business of project operations and forget all the "talk." Project participants frequently are opposed to, or at least reluctant about, spending time on evaluation. They feel it is a diversion from their main task. In a similar vein, the sponsoring agency may severely restrict the amount of money that can be made available for evaluation, considering that such expenditures border on the unnecessary or even the "luxurious," especially if they involve trips abroad for special evaluation personnel.

An even more severe difficulty in following an orderly evaluation program arises from the very intricate system of interpersonal relations that develop after a project has been under way for some months. Those who are introducing change will normally try to push as rapidly as possible. They will have a series of informal relationships with host country personnel and they may come to view a formal evaluation as a threat to the fabric of relationships they have established. They may be fearful that an assessment of project progress will be unduly critical of host country personnel, thus destroying certain opportunities for "breakthroughs" that they have been patiently developing. Informal agreements to introduce certain changes in the near future may have been reached, and an evaluation, even if the results are not made public, may call attention to the need for such changes in a manner that will be detrimental to the chances of their introduction.

There is a strong case against public evaluation of any and all aspects of a project. Any assessment must be made with due regard for the sensitivities present in a project which, if catered to, may result in more rapid change. However, much of the possible embarrassment can be avoided by building in a plan for evaluation at the time the initial contract is negotiated. If all parties know that systematic assessment of project progress and prospects is to take place regularly, and that each of them is to participate in the process, then much of the unhappiness associated with intensive evaluation is avoided.

Evaluations are centrally concerned with the purposes of a project and the strategies that have been and can be followed to achieve them. Those assigned to carry out the assessment may find that the objectives and aims of the project have been made unduly rigid by the contract or in practice by project administrators, so that alternative or additional objectives have not been considered carefully as the project has evolved. Project evaluators should have clear terms of reference in going beyond stated objectives.

The state of knowledge concerning major social change is such that no single detailed strategy or set of strategies can be considered as the correct one for achieving prescribed ends. Thus the evaluator may view the strategy and methods pursued critically and suggest certain alternatives. The reaction of the participants may be negative; they prefer the existing ones. It is difficult for either to prove that they are correct. Until our knowledge of social change is much farther advanced, evaluations of strategies should be made in terms of possible alternatives rather than in terms of prescriptions, except in rare instances.

None of the personal and technical problems of evaluation may be nearly as crucial a factor in successful project assessment as the political problems of the host country and the United States government. One or both of the governments may not welcome an open and frank assessment. Evaluations that are critical of the host government or the financial sponsor may jeopardize the continued existence of the project. Evaluations whose results or recommendations run counter to the prevailing school of thought on technical assistance in the country mission may disrupt relations between the mission and the university. On occasion, such risks must be taken if project integrity is to be maintained. On other occasions, a "softer" way around must be found. Support for evaluations that are favorable to a group or agency is never hard to find. A public evaluation coupled with a "restricted" supplement may avoid some of the risks.

Accomplishments to Date

The main burden of the present paper has been to outline the principal problems encountered in conducting systematic evaluations of university technical assistance projects abroad. Increasingly, evaluations will depend in part upon expectations of impact, which in turn will rise as universities gain more skill and experience in their overseas activities. Therefore, some reflections on the overall performance of the universities overseas are presented. These are primarily impressions, rather than research conclusions, since no large-scale evaluation of American universities abroad has been made in the last several years. In analyzing the kinds of impact made through university work overseas, it should first be noted that the American universities themselves have been among the most affected by these efforts, more affected than some of the host country institutions.

Fifteen years ago American universities were unskilled in the ways of technical assistance abroad. Looking back over the events of the last decade and a half, I believe that the most striking thing about university contracts overseas is the vast experience, both institutional and individual, that has been built up. Today, American universities are far better organized to carry out projects in other countries, and many professors expect and want to participate in them. It is no longer the lone entrepreneur, somewhat scorned by his colleagues, who promotes a university project. Instead, an office of international programs exists at many large universities with recognized and competent leadership, backed by an experienced faculty and administration.

Generally speaking, the field missions of universities are more ably led and composed of stronger people than in the early days. Their relations with both financial sponsors and host country nationals have markedly improved. This is probably due to some-what greater sophistication about the intricacies of technical assistance, as well as a more mature approach to working out initial plans and contract details. The universities can strike a harder and more favorable bargain than previously.

While all the early technical assistance efforts were carried out by single universities, it is increasingly common to have consortia of universities accepting such responsibilities. This has permitted a greater diversification of contracts at any one university, how-ever large it may be, and has also permitted smaller institutions to become involved. There are dozens of such consortia today carrying on one or another type of international program.

There has been major accommodative impact upon American universities from overseas contracts. The net result has been to enable the universities to carry out such assignments much more effectively than in the past. They have more closely related their overseas activities to the regular on-going campus programs. While perfect adjustment can never be expected, a significant change has taken place on American campuses and in teams sent to the field, as a result of project feedback.

The impact on the host country is to be defined in terms of the achievement of long-term goals, intermediate aims, and specific objectives.

Long-Term Goals

The broadest purposes underlying university technical assist-ance projects abroad are by no means solely achieved through these projects alone. Host country political, economic, educa-tional, and cultural development has innumerable facets, and university projects abroad are very small elements in the total effort being made to hasten development. Some of the graduates of the institutions that American universities have helped to es-tablish or strengthen are playing key roles in certain phases of industrial or agricultural development in their respective coun-tries. There is more development-consciousness among host uni-versity faculties than previously. However, the main development effort must, of necessity, come from many large undertakings, and not from the relatively small American university projects.

The objectives of American or host country foreign policy may be advanced through university contracts, but it is again obvious that this is not the major way in which such policy is advanced, even though foreign policy considerations may be important for a particular project. To the extent that host institutions assisted by American universities are made to work more effectively, the threat of communism is definitely reduced. But there are no field data that would indicate that university projects play a key role in combating communism. Nor does anyone seriously feel they should. Friends are made for the United States by American professors working abroad. Lasting professional friendships have been a notable result, and a true international colleagueship is being forged by these projects and other instruments that bring scholars together from different countries. Still, academic friendships affect the American image abroad in a relatively small way.

A major accomplishment in regard to broad long-term goals lies in the area of advancing knowledge. In the last two decades, a new dimension has been added to the old "comparative" studies that were undertaken at universities. Only part of the change lies in a greater concentration on non-European countries. The more significant change is in regard to furthering knowledge that is not culture-bound. In the social sciences and the professions, broad new areas of research have been pursued. Prominent among the leaders have been American professors who have served overseas on technical assistance projects. The projects themselves have made somewhat disappointing contributions to research, but the host country and American professors involved have had their interest sparked in advancing knowledge cross-culturally.

Intermediate Aims

The intermediate aims of university projects overseas largely center on institution-building and target groups. University contract programs are commonly associated with institution-building objectives. A majority of them encompass such aims. Frequently an institution is established at the time that technical assistance is sought; under these circumstances project personnel have a responsibility to give real life to the new institution so that it can perform a significant and lasting function. In some cases, university personnel are to start from scratch in developing plans for a new organization which has yet to be authorized.

Two notable trends in regard to institution-building mark university projects abroad in recent years. First, there is far greater recognition of the significance of successful institution-building by American personnel. Universities often describe their entire task abroad in these terms. Second, there is far less tendency to transplant American institutions and more concern with developing an organization that will be adapted to the host country environment. This is not to say that all projects have been successful in institution-building. The ways of social innovation are difficult and tortuous. Still, as a whole, American universities have achieved a modest degree of success in this area.

Impact on target groups is difficult to ascertain. The more removed target groups are from project operations, the more diluted is project impact and the greater is impact from other factors. While few systematic assessments have been made of project impact on remote target groups, it is evident that greater attention is being given to the training of trainers than was true of the first decade of university experience abroad. At that time, initial project concern was in getting the job done, and it appeared to be easiest and quickest if American professors taught host country students directly. Gradually, university project personnel came to realize the powerful multiplication effect of training the trainers and at the same time institution-building by establishing more effective educational and training organizations for target groups. Universities began to switch their emphasis. The trend is by no means complete, however. There are still a few American universities who are trying to reach target groups directly by sending their staff members abroad to teach—and not just to teach as a planned demonstration or as temporary substitutes until host staff be trained. There are many universities who do not plan a systematic spread effect through creating a series of institutions that would in turn have educational or training functions. If a medical school is being established, are suitable institutes also being established around the country for training para-health personnel? If a school of education is being established, are suitable institutes also being established around the country for elementary and secondary teacher training? If a school of public administration is being established, are suitable in-service training units also being established in the several ministries and provinces?

Specific Objectives

In some ways, the most frustrating aspects of the impact of American university technical assistance projects abroad have been in regard to the accomplishment of certain specific objectives. On paper, it would seem that these would be the easiest of all to achieve because they are relatively discrete and specific. But perhaps because they are so specific they impinge very sharply upon host country personnel. Teaching techniques and study habits of students, especially, have a kind of finality about them as far as the host country participants are concerned that may arouse a resistance to change that is greater than that accorded more sweeping but less personal change.

Of the several specific objectives of university projects, the most commonly found are changes in courses and curricula and modification of teaching techniques. They are to be found in nearly all university projects. Course change and curriculum building are among the specific objectives most completely achieved. They are also the least personal. Normally, the contract authorizing a university project specifies the kind of curriculum development that is to take place. Consequently, all parties to the agreement have advance knowledge that some project activity is to take place in this area. When a new professional school or university is to be established, new courses and curricula are a natural part of the total effort, except when ministries of education rigidly prescribe them. Even where new institutions have not been created, course innovation has been frequent. Four trends have been evident: the establishment of curricula for new professional schools, the introduction of broad general education courses, experimentation with courses stressing the application of knowledge to practical problems of the host country, and the creation of courses employing new approaches to mathematics and the sciences.

Nearly every project includes some provision for training of host country faculty members—in the host country, in the United States, or both. Experiences with these training programs have been more impressive in terms of numbers than in their effect on the nature of instruction at the host institution. Of course, where a new institution has been established, such training programs have usually been the means by which the bulk of the staff has been recruited. From this point of view, at least, it can be said that these training programs have been successful. There have been "leakages," that is, not all the returned professors have stayed at their assigned tasks at the host university. The fact remains that a considerable number of trained persons have been added to the working force of the host countries through university projects abroad.

The teaching techniques of host country professors have changed very, very slowly considering the time and effort that have been expended on this matter. The discussion technique has been the focus of much attention, but the lecture method still prevails overwhelmingly. The use of reading materials has been another great point of stress, but the newly established libraries still go largely unused by the students. The examination system has proved itself highly resistant to change. Some laboratory and field work has been introduced, however.

The study habits of host country students have also been largely unaffected by most university projects. In countries where both professors and students are part time, it is difficult to make any inroads on teaching techniques and study habits— two sides of the same coin. Students study in a manner that will get them through the university satisfactorily. If the examination system is not changed, study habits of students will not change either. If the professor remains aloof, the students will not take the initiative to question him in or out of class. If the number of courses that students are required to take remains high, there will be no time or incentive to read in the library.

Thus while institutions have been built, courses and curricula established, and professors sent abroad for advanced degrees so that the teaching staffs have expanded both in numbers and quality, the core relation between student and professor has proved to be quite impervious to outside influence. It may be a long time before much progress can be reported on this front.

Evaluation of university technical assistance projects abroad should take place in the context of what has been learned and accomplished to date. A project that was exceedingly successful in terms of the conditions of the early 1950's might be considered very unsuccessful in light of what can be expected today. As our experience and skills improve, our expectations of project results must be raised. The process of accelerating social change becomes ever more demanding.

John F. Hilliard

A Perspective
on International Development

Twenty years and 100 billion dollars later, the United States government is wondering what it bought for its foreign aid money and what lessons it can learn for the years ahead. So are the United Nations and its specialized agencies, the highly developed countries of Europe, and those private foundations able and willing to take a hand in the international development game. All are pretty sure they have not got just what they bargained for and are not sure they like what they got. Neither are the underdeveloped countries. Just past mid-point in the Development Decade, there are worldwide second thoughts on what international development is, how it is achieved, how long it takes, and what it costs.

These second thoughts are not really new; the difference is that they are now so universally expressed. For the United States a slow-burning fuse led to the events of late 1963 and 1964, when such time-tested champions of foreign aid as Senator Fulbright and (then) Senator Humphrey publicly declared their lack of support for the foreign aid program as proposed by the Administration. Already over halfway through the fiscal year, it appeared for a time that the revolt on Capitol Hill was so complete that there would be no foreign aid appropriation for 1964. The same kind of atmosphere has continued to exist, particularly in the Senate.

Meanwhile, back on the campuses of the United States, a long smoldering resentment of the policies and methods of the aid agency had led the AID administrator to commission Education and World Affairs to make a major study of AID and the universities, directed by John W. Gardner, then president of the Carnegie Corporation of New York. The Gardner report was issued in April 1964 and the McGovern Bill was introduced a few months later, both proposing radical innovations in the policies, organization, and funding of the technical assistance aspects of foreign aid.

During 1964 the major private organizations engaged in overseas development reviewed their activities, surveyed the prospective future of official foreign aid activities, and prepared to adjust to a variety of new equations none of which could be predicted with certainty.

When the Foreign Aid Bill of 1965 was served up to the Senate Committee on Foreign Relations, the chairman characterized it as "garbage" and for a time refused to serve as floor leader for it. By a narrow margin, legislation was avoided which would have put a two-year termination on the program and required the Administration to submit radically new proposals for any future program.

In February 1966 President Johnson sent to Congress a Special Message on International Education, and the International Education Act of 1966 was introduced in the Senate and in the House, and later enacted. This far-reaching legislation adds an important new dimension to the role of education in international development and provides for the development of American educational institutions to better serve this purpose. It provides as well for mobilizing federal departments and agencies having educational functions relevant to international development. The traditional functions of AID are to be given a greater educational emphasis.

In the light of these developments, it seems reasonable to assume that within the remaining three years of the Development Decade, international development will enter a new phase conceptually, organizationally, and financially. In so doing, it will pose major new problems and opportunities for official agencies of both donor and underdeveloped countries, for private agencies engaged in overseas development, and for American universities interested in the development field. It will also produce new concepts and relationships for the architects of development who are struggling with one of the world's most intractable problems, with inadequate resources and tools.

The following observations bear without dogmatism on many of these matters. They are designed to produce discussion, not a position; thought, not agreement.

A Brief Background

The U.S. official foreign aid program figures centrally in any consideration of experience in this field, because it has been and is the largest administered by any nation or combination of nations. The combined technical assistance investments of all the private foundations and voluntary organizations, important as they are, in monetary terms represent only a fraction of the over 100 billion dollars expended to date on foreign aid by the federal government. For example, the Ford Foundation overseas development program, begun in 1951, had as of September 1965 made a total commitment of 333.8 million dollars or .33 percent of the official U.S. expenditure. (It is, of course, a much larger fraction of federal expenditures for *technical assistance,* which in recent years have been about 200 million dollars annually.)

By its very size, diversity, and evolution, the AID program has tended to bring into its orbit the activities of private organizations and to exercise a major gravitational pull on those of the United Nations and its specialized agencies. Even so, the aid authorization requested for 1967 represents only 2 percent of the federal budget for 1967 compared with 12 percent for 1950. The Advisory Committee on Private Enterprise in Foreign Aid pointed out last year that the 2 billion dollars the United States injects into the economies of 72 countries annually amounts to 1.44 dollars per person.

Appraisals of the overall effects of external resources on the developing countries vary widely. The official U.S. dialectic before Congress has held that it is a basic feature of an effective international security system and that it has served this purpose well, events in the Caribbean, East Asia, and elsewhere notwithstanding. There is a lengthening list of "graduates" alleged to represent proof of the fundamental importance of U.S. assistance in helping poorer countries reach a point of self-sustaining growth.

Perhaps a more valid appraisal is found in the fact that many of the underdeveloped countries have made real and visible progress. To anyone who has worked in these countries during the past decade, this is a persuasive point: there is undeniably a change in the climate of development, a perceivable connection with the future, better-trained people, purposeful institutions, physical infrastructure, that were not there ten years ago. There also remain massive and enduring problems in all these areas, plus increasingly evident problems in population growth, urbanization, political maturity, and systems of communications essential to nationhood and international cooperation. Few, these days, would argue that foreign aid has made the donors popular with the aid recipients, or that the underdeveloped countries have thereby found a common ground for mutual help.

Even the "success" stories like Greece, Turkey, Mexico, and Taiwan are marred by burgeoning growth of population, economic isolation of large numbers of their people, or by political instability that threatens to undercut the gains they have made. Efforts at regional cooperation for development have met with recent success in Central America, but with failure in the collapse of federations in the Caribbean, East Africa, and Asia.

In the past few years there has been a growing concern on the part of the donor nations about the inadequacy of self-help and discipline on the part of the developing countries in mobilizing their internal resources for development and in effecting economic and social reforms. It is a fact that, in many countries, projected reforms have lagged and internal resources have not come up to anticipated standards. Pessimists point to the fact that since 1950 the food-population balance has deteriorated and the economic gap between the developed and underdeveloped countries has become relatively wider. This, they say, has resulted in a growing cynicism in the developing countries, likely to lead to a destructive wave of antagonism against the fortunate few wealthy nations.

The central concern of serious advocates of international development was well expressed by Professor Abdus Salam of Imperial College, London:

> Never in the history of mankind has a change happened all at once. The one great change of the first half of this century—the passing of the colonial age—was the culmination of fifty years of crusading. In most places it all started with a few men, whose passionate fury first overwhelmed their own peoples and then succeeded in rousing the liberal conscience of their captors, bringing home to them also the utter economic futility of holding down an unwilling people. This is the normal process of change. What makes me worried is that no such thing has yet happened in the underdeveloped world so far as the harder crusade against poverty is concerned. And in a few places where realization has come, it has not been purposeful enough yet to bring down the internal social and organizational barriers, nor to be able to defy external pressures.

The underdeveloped countries also have strong opinions on the effect of foreign aid on development. Many believe that in the aggregate, the developed nations of the world have never provided enough capital or technical assistance to give them any reasonable prospect of self-sustaining growth, in national terms, within an acceptable time period. They feel that the donor nations have been unwilling to assure a fair price structure for the international commodity market—the one major resource the developing nations have for financing their plans. Undoubtedly two of the dominant problems faced by the developing countries are the uncertain prospect of their export earnings and the increasing amount of money needed annually to service their external debt.

There is also an increasing feeling on the part of the developing countries that the donors attempt a major intervention in their national policies without a commensurate contribution to the development process. Many feel that the timing and magnitude of reforms proposed by the donors are unrealistic and that "reform" represents an incorrect premise on which to base development aid. Some advance the position that concessional aid from the wealthy countries is related to the historic disadvantages they experienced through the end of the colonial period.

That the private foundations engaged in overseas development have escaped many of the foregoing problems is only in part attributable to their virtue. They do not have to enter into the arena of political relations at home or with foreign governments in the way required of official agencies. Their objectives, as well as their funds, are more limited, their activities more selective, and their commitments more flexible and for longer periods than most of those effected under government to government terms. These are the natural increments to the effectiveness of private American institutions with overseas development interests and capabilities.

The foundations thus far appear to have been more effective pragmatically than they have in contributing to the growth of a philosophy or doctrine of international development. This is understandable since a good deal of pragmatic experience in any new field is necessary before synthesizing concepts and principles is possible, particularly in the social sciences. However, in the decade ahead, the foundations should assume a major role in creating an overall philosophy and set of principles by which international development can be conducted and evaluated.

The "institutions in the middle," the universities and private non-profit corporations, have undoubtedly played an increasingly important role in overseas development. The particular disabilities under which the universities have labored (and, in considerable part, non-university scholarly institutions) were rather definitely spelled out by Gardner in *AID and the Universities*. Many of his observations bearing specifically on AID-university relations are more or less directly applicable to foundation-university relations.

Thus far the partnership between overseas development agencies, public and private, and the universities has been, generally speaking, a spotty and makeshift affair. In the first years of the development program, the universities were regarded by official agencies as "job shops" for specific development assignments designed by aid agency personnel. More recently, they have been caught in the anomalous position of being admonished to make long-term institutional commitments to participate in an officially proclaimed "short-term" overseas aid program. The limited definition of development has made it difficult for a university to involve itself in overseas work *as a university*. Under provisions contemplated by the International Education Act of 1966, a more favorable environment for university participation in international development may be expected to evolve. However, the process of organizing for and learning how to enter effectively into international development must engage the best thought of the universities for at least another decade.

As evidenced by the foregoing observations, even the normal clarity of hindsight fails to give us an adequate impression of the achievements and failures of international development in the past fifteen years, but little by little we seem to be beginning to understand why. Perhaps the most important problem is that we are examining in a very short time focus one of the most novel, complex, and difficult worldwide endeavors in all history. The passing of the colonial age, to use Professor Salam's phrase, released into the world an enormous amount of political, economic, and social energy with only primitive mechanisms through which it could be absorbed and used, and found a spectrum-wide variety among the nations in time, concepts, technology, and institutions.

Undoubtedly a second and central reason for our difficulty in trying to appraise our experience and reshape our course is that all participants in the development process have been going through a disorderly apprenticeship for the exacting craft of development. Early assumptions about the nature of development, its key problems, time frame, and scale of effort required for success, have had to be modified extensively. Development institutions and resources have had to be built from scratch in both donor and developing countries.

Third, the definition of development has essentially been cast in the mold of economics and physical technology, with only limited recognition of the social amenities required for life to approach an acceptable human level. This definition has persisted in spite of the fact that a large part of our experience thus far indicates that the problems of development are as deeply rooted in political, intellectual, and cultural structures as they are in economics and technology.

Finally, it seems increasingly clear that the scale of effort applied to development, from both internal and external resources, has not been of such magnitude as to give any reasonable prospect of contemporary success for most countries. Moreover, these resources have not always been concentrated on the crucial problems; they have usually been dispersed over a great range of projects and "program areas" lacking any competent design for development of the country based upon scientific knowledge of its real development potential.

These observations are not meant to be pessimistic; if we have not had all the right answers in the first year of this epochal enterprise in development, at least we appear to have earned the time for reflection and another try.

A Perspective on the Next Decade

In portraying a problem as pervasive and crucial to the world as development, there is a temptation to use somewhat desperate terms. The situation indeed has desperate implications and these may well be more ominous than we can now perceive. It cannot be taken for granted that development as a worldwide phenomenon will necessarily succeed. In fact recent history gives chilling glimpses of how nations may meet disaster on the road to success. But desperation is not good counsel. Even one of our gloomier philosophers has observed, "Hope is at least as intelligent as despair." It is therefore necessary to assume that, during the next decade, disaster will not overtake development in any general sense, and that the central thrust of the development effort of the past decade has a basic validity and should continue.

It seems clear to many that if its chances of success are to be enhanced very significant changes must be made in the conceptions, scale, and methodology of that effort. Perhaps the most fundamental change required is that we greatly broaden the con-

cept of development to include all aspects of *national* development, including pursuit of goals which are political and intellectual, psychological and conceptual, creative and cultural—as well
as economic, scientific, and social.

Despite considerable lip service to such a broader definition,
so far the *effective* conceptions of development have been defined,
conducted, and evaluated essentially in economic terms—per
capita income, gross national product, and so on. Even education
has been conceived of and justified by economic criteria despite
the rather reluctant recognition that it is also a "consumer good."
Growth of human skill and leadership have become "human
capital formation." It is becoming increasingly clear that as
valuable as economics is as a method of planning, conducting,
and evaluating certain aspects of development, more has been
asked of it than the state of the art can produce when we address
the problem of *national* development. National development has
as one of its major goals the increase in quantity and improvement in distribution of economic goods. But this is only one of
the goals and its achievement depends very heavily on the realization of other goals which are wholly non-economic in any direct
or immediate sense.

National development requires a reasonable synthesis in all
fields of political, intellectual, economic, social, and cultural endeavor. Beyond these, it requires a widely diffused acceptance of
a structure of ideas and a system of symbols which facilitate communications and provide an effective sense of national identity, an
intelligent respect for the country's own cultural antecedents with
an orientation toward modernization. Although not easy to define
and very difficult to quantify in economic terms, the ideas men
hold about their relationships to each other essentially determine
whether there can be created either a viable economic system or
a nation-state. The will to develop is demonstrably more important than any other single factor in achieving development, and
it would be difficult to show that national development, in the
sense it is defined here, has ever been achieved without strong
motivations unrelated to economic self-interest.

A redefinition of development that fully considers non-economic factors can have very important conceptual and operational values. In conceptual terms, it adds vision to planning and helps reconcile traditional values with future aims. Operationally, it would place the developed and underdeveloped nations in a more equalitarian relationship, in which they both have much to give as well as to receive. In program terms, it would make possible the mobilization of important resources for development in both developed and underdeveloped countries which are now regarded as extraneous or only marginally related. As a specific instance, it would permit the proper involvement of the vast resources of the educational and cultural institutions of the United States as well as those directly related to economic development.

To give effect to this broader concept of development, it is essential that a new image of foreign aid be created and supported by policy and legislation as a permanent, stable, professionally managed, American contribution to worldwide development. It seems unlikely that we are still lacking experience or national character upon which to build a permanent structure for participating in the great constructive endeavors of our time. The publicly made arguments for the official U.S. assistance programs have often reflected little credit on our motivations and certainly have not aroused the admiration or confidence of the aided nations. It is doubtful that anyone takes seriously any longer the allegation that American aid to Upper Volta or Ecuador, or to much more powerful countries for that matter, serves to increase our national security in any significant way.

It would seem time that the issue of moral responsibility and membership in the family of nations be faced squarely. Certainly there can be no Great Society without a great moral purpose and a firm commitment to the improvement of the lot of man. This does not imply an endless commitment to foreign aid as we have known it, but to an evolving relationship characterized by "transition" rather than "phase-out." It would seem reasonable to think of participation in development as extending through the whole spectrum of relations from aid given on a heavily concessional basis to full economic, political, and cultural partnership. Indeed, if we accept the fact that the highly developed countries will probably continue to widen the economic and technological gap between themselves and the developing countries, no concept of termination of assistance appears realistic. It is entirely realistic to conceive of the relationship as one of growing reciprocity. An aid agency and program of this character would, for the first time, provide a major role in development for universities and other institutions of learning; a role clearly defined, adequately funded, and properly coordinated within the government.

The process of development is much more than a mobilization of economic resources—it requires reconstruction of societies in a broad sense. And in these terms, development becomes more closely identified with the historic mission of the university in the development, diffusion, and application of knowledge in all fields. The International Education Act of 1966 promises to provide a significant improvement in the relationship of educational institutions to development. Nevertheless, the organizational design for development and management of international education and the foreign aid program is still far from clear.

American universities have already made very significant contributions to development when they have been engaged in such a way as to maintain their functions as teaching and research institutions. And it should not be forgotten that this involvement has provided tremendous enrichment for American education. A more effective, long-term commitment to development by our universities can do more to promote our interest in and effective understanding of other peoples and cultures than any other single force. This makes for immeasurably better education for its own sake; but with the kind of world in which we now live, it can make the difference between success and failure, not just of the developing countries but of the whole human race.

In performing an expanded role in international education, American institutions must face the fact that education is not essentially an export commodity. Special and competent efforts must be made to help establish strategically placed centers of learning in each region of the world. These centers should have as their objective the creation of environments and opportunities for a quality of intellectual, scientific, and creative work comparable to the best to be found in any highly developed country. These can provide scholarly bases from which American institutions can make their most important contribution in the developing countries; but more important they can become a major countervailing force to the attraction to the highly developed countries and institutions of the most talented men and women of the developing countries. It is essential and through such centers possible to convert the "brain drain" into an effective process of internationalizing knowledge, to the great advantage of all countries participating.

There are already institutions and areas where such centers of learning are emerging. New arrangements are being worked out for joint professorships between institutions, research fellowships, and a variety of other measures whereby first-class scholars can remain active in their own countries and at the same time participate in the scholarly life of the world community. It may well be that an international labor market will have to be created in terms of salaries and other incentives in order to deploy the skills essential to development in an effective way.

It seems increasingly clear that the the scale of effort going into development must be very significantly increased if success is to be achieved within the time likely to be available. For the United States this means that special encouragement must be given to private enterprise to undertake serious and sustained efforts, under its own leadership, to become progressively more effective in contributing to international development. As noted by the recent report of the Committee on Private Enterprise in Foreign Aid: "There is a huge gap between what the less-developed countries need for a tolerable rate of growth, and what they are likely to get. As far as their capital needs are concerned . . . the size of the gap is staggering—between 5 billion dollars and 20 billion dollars annually." Unless the unique talents and resources of American private enterprise are tapped much more effectively, it will be virtually impossible to mount the development effort on a scale calculated to give promise of real success.

Repeated efforts on the part of the government and industry to effect a larger contribution to development by private enterprise remain disappointing, in spite of the fact that American industry has an unparalleled capability in the fields of technology, organization, management, and finance. It is difficult to escape the impression that private enterprise everywhere, including the United States, has failed to see its historic stake in the success of worldwide development, and that therefore it has failed to show courage or inventiveness in contributing to it.

The growing capacity of the developing countries to absorb both capital and technical assistance, plus what appears to be some lessening of hypersensitivity to foreign investors, would seem to offer private enterprise an opportunity to study in depth its potential role and to devise the minimum conditions under which industry could contribute to development programs without unreasonable risk to the proper interests of either the participating companies or the developing country. Such an effort should preferably be organized and financed by private enterprise institutions through some structure such as the Committee for Economic Development, and in concert with independent research organizations such as the Brookings Institution.

During the coming decade, development plans must move from a series of tactical operations to strategic designs based upon known development potentials. This means that major emphasis must be given to scientific and systematic studies of resource potentials using the advanced technology now available for this purpose.

Probably there is not in existence today a plan for development which is based upon anything approaching a realistic inventory of development assets and liabilities, human or material. This has necessarily brought about the wide use of *ad hoc* planning based on economic targets or hopes rather than upon realistic development potentials. Resource data just have not been available. But the plans of the past few years must be improved and projected through the next ten or twenty years, and therefore must become much more realistic in terms of resource inventories and uses than the limited tactical exercise of the past.

The logical elaboration of development potentials must also take into account the possibilities of regional combines, export earnings, technology, manpower, and external assistance needed in some or all of these areas. Obviously all these increasingly complex planning problems, with their necessarily longer lead-time requirements, put a high premium on a new era in development planning, more solidly based on what is doable in the short-term but consistent with a long-term resource mobilization program.

Inventorying of resources is by no means the only use to which advanced technology should be applied, as it is highly relevant to many of the most crucial development problems.

During the past years there has been a wide divergence of opinion in and outside the developed countries regarding employment of the "leading edge" of science in underdeveloped countries. The social scientists have generally held that modernization of primitive or traditional societies is a grassroots operation and must recapitulate the slow growth of skills and institutions of the developed countries. Increasingly, the advocates of development have argued that acceptance of this doctrine is, in effect, acceptance of ultimate defeat, since the time for recapitulating a hundred years of trial and error is simply not available; and that the only real prospect of achieving such goals as food production, education, health, population control, housing, and communications is a radical and purposeful resort to science and technology.

It seems curious that with the spectacular advances in science and technology so little has been done even to *investigate* their potential for development, to say nothing of employing them experimentally and purposefully in critical fields. It is true that work of significance has been done in agriculture and health. More recently, science has made and is making major contributions in the field of human fertility. However, employment of science for producing large quantities of fresh water is still economically infeasible. The world food deficit continues to grow, chronic ill health remains one of the monumental impediments to development, and population growth has shown little, if any, decline in any underdeveloped country.

In spite of the obvious availability of major advances in the technology of communications, transportation, natural resource identification, low-cost environmentally adapted housing, nutrition, endemic disease control, and education, only rarely is the most advanced knowledge brought to bear on an effective scale. Surely, advanced systems analysis and data processing techniques would be worth trying in selected countries or regional groupings of countries.

It should, of course, be made clear that what is proposed is *not* a large-scale, crash program of advanced technology for development. What is proposed is a larger and sustained *investigation and testing* of the potentialities of science and technology for all fields of development. Where findings are promising vigorous efforts should be made to shorten the time between favorable tests and wide-scale application.

It is also important that increasing efforts be made, through the use of advanced technology, to attack large-scale environmental or geographic problems in development. There are impressive examples around the world of successful application of strategic planning and science to large-scale resource potentials. The Tennessee Valley Authority in the United States is a classic example, but rarely duplicated even where opportunities exist. A more recent example is the Rice Research Institute in Asia; projected Institutes of Tropical Agriculture, both arid and humid, may be other examples. The Aswan Valley Regional Development Authority in Egypt and the Khuzestan River Valley Development Project in Iran are others. In the field of health, malaria eradication is a partial demonstration of the potential.

But the concept of large-scale development based on a major resource (such as a great forest in Liberia, minerals in the Ivory Coast) or assaulting regional or environmental problems on a massive scale has been slow to take shape. This is, of course, in part because of the inherent difficulty of the problems, international frontiers, political sensitivities, and valid differences in attitudes toward development. But our growing experience is encouraging enough to justify (as in the case of science and technology) a larger and sustained *investigation* of these potentials during the coming years.

One of the many extraordinary things about development is the difficulty of understanding what causes it; how it can be accelerated; what is an acceptable or desirable rate of change; what is the relationship between physical and social technology; and, in a larger sense, how political and economic systems of different sizes, shapes, and speeds can be geared to each other so that the machinery of world development can turn.

Equally mysterious is why so far such little effort has been devoted to finding answers to these obviously crucial questions.

For the first thirteen years of U.S. aid to underdeveloped countries, the aid agency had no organized program of research in the phenomena of development. In 1963 it established such a program, with 6 million dollars in funds, or about .003 percent of the AID annual expenditure. Although this original amount has risen, it still bears no adequate relationship to the size of the expenditures for development. The international agencies and the private foundations have also given a low priority to research in the process and dynamics of development.

It is an encouraging fact that the neglect of the past is gradually being relieved by a larger, broader, and more imaginative research program, both public and private; competence in this field is growing, in the underdeveloped as well as in the developed countries. Development, however, is not a state but a process, and this puts a continuing premium on keeping an evolving research program geared to the unfolding realities of today and tomorrow. And if this research can be even moderately successful, it not only can significantly accelerate development but save much more money than it costs.

Finally during the next decade, the underdeveloped and the developed nations must forge a true partnership for development.

For the past fifteen years, aid to the developing countries has been assumed by donor and, to some extent, by recipient nations to be essentially a one-way flow. Those who supported aid on grounds of national self-interest regarded the gain to the United States as explicitly strategic in military or political terms. Those who supported the program as a moral and human imperative implicitly regarded it as essentially a spiritual gain. In the first, the developing nation is regarded as a pawn, in the second, as a beneficiary; in neither is there a clear concept of the developing country as a partner in a great human enterprise which transcends the national goals of both participants.

There is, of course, an element of reality in conceiving of aid, intelligently administered, as having both strategic and spiritual value. But it undeniably carries the implication of a superior-subordinate relationship—the "advanced" nation helping the "retarded" nation, at some net cost and disadvantage to itself. In this context the term "advanced" usually has been regarded as applying to the whole spectrum of achievement rather than to political institutions, economics, and technology. It has often been overlooked that the achievements of the "underdeveloped" countries in the fields of basic science, religion, the arts, and the humanities compare favorably with those of the most "advanced" nations. In addition, during the past two decades, there has emerged an elite group in most of the developing countries which is fully comparable to the best in the donor countries in the fields crucial to modernization and development.

The emerging partnership for development, therefore, must be based upon an understanding and acceptance by all participants in the development process that they all have much to give and much to receive, and that, though they play different roles, the common enterprise in which they are engaged is the main business of man in this century.

American Council on Education

Logan Wilson, President

The American Council on Education, founded in 1918, is a *council* of educational organizations and institutions. Its purpose is to advance education and educational methods through comprehensive voluntary and cooperative action on the part of American educational associations, organizations, and institutions.